FRYING PORK CHOPS NAKED

ANOTHER POCKETFUL OF FUNNY LIFE STORIES

ERIC V. LITSKY

ISBN: 979-8-9883776-0-3 (print)

Book Cover by Arlene Soto, Intricate Designs

Formatting and Publishing Consulting by Bannon River Books, LLC

First Edition

CONTENTS

PROLOGUE

America's Pastime

S ome games you win. And some games you lose. And some games get rained out. But you have to dress for all of them.

Or you could find yourself naked and wet.

In my first book, *Harry Would Be So Proud,* I wrote several stories of how baseball weaved in and out of my life. How it brought me close to my father. How my Uncle Jack took me to my first NY Mets game at the Polo Grounds. It was the second game of their inaugural season. They were terrible. They lost. But it made me a lifelong fan.

I wrote how I finagled World Series tickets a decade later. I naively called the owner of the Mets directly. I then slept through the entire series with a nasty case of the flu.

I wrote how my grandfather who knew nothing of baseball took me to a double header which he later referred to as a 'double headache.'

Baseball has been a constant in my life since my earliest days at PS 176.

Until I took up smoking and girls, I collected baseball cards. I would spend my entire allowance on them. A pack of 6 cards included a flat stick of bubble gum. It was only a nickel.

I read the stats on the back of each card wondering how my stats would stack up when I got to the majors. I treasured my Mickey Mantle, Willie Mays, Hank Aaron. The great stars of my day. Their baseball cards were kept in mint condition.

My first foray into gambling was flipping baseball cards. Holding a card at my side I would flip it down attempting to land each or most of them either on heads or tails.

My opponent would need to match whatever I threw down. There were usually five cards gambled in each match. It was 'winner take all.' And then we'd go again. I won much more than I lost. I had many hundreds of baseball cards in a large box in my bedroom closet.

My baseball cards from those days would be worth thousands of dollars today. But you already know what happened. My mother threw them out when I left for college.

When my first grandchild was born, I began making annual purchases of an entire rack of Topps Baseball cards. Every card printed. All 700 of them. I had hopes that one of my grandchildren would be drawn to collecting baseball cards. Or at least cashing them out when they are ready for college.

It is now almost twelve years later, and I can't wait to get these damn cards out of my house.

My dream was to play professional baseball. Our local baseball field backed up to the Cross Island Parkway in Queens.

As a young teenager I could easily clear the 15 ft outfield fence, lofting a home run into highway traffic. It is hard to imagine that no one was killed. But that was New York in the 1960's. No one thought that far ahead.

My high school was Andrew Jackson High School, a large urban school in St. Albans, Queens. We had 4,000 students. Its baseball field behind the school was run down. Broken glass. Large divots in the outfield.

These were not the manicured fields found on Long Island on the other side of the Cross Island Parkway. It separated the lower middle-class borough of Queens from the nouveau-riche communities of Nassau County.

By the time I got to high school I was a very good defensive catcher with a strong and accurate arm. I could hit a ball a long way if it were thrown straight down the middle of the plate.

But my knees buckled when I was thrown a curveball.

A curveball is thrown in close to the batter. Its spin allows it to curve over the plate into the strike zone. Great hitters can pick up the spin of the ball as it leaves the pitcher's hand, and then smack it as it curves over the plate.

I was not a great hitter.

I don't know how many times I stood at the plate hearing the umpire shout, *"Strike three!"*

I spent most of the season riding the bench. It was there where my dream of playing pro ball died.

But that didn't stop me from being a lifelong fan.

From the ages of 12 through much of college, I attended opening day at Shea Stadium watching my beloved NY Mets. Usually, they would lose. I would cut out of school with a few friends. It would be a day to remember.

School was chaotic. No one missed us. Upper deck seating was inexpensive. A few dollars got us in. Hot dogs were only 40 cents. We'd stomp hard on the small mustard packages. Sending a stream of yellow mustard down to the mezzanine seats below.

Of course, there was the opening day when my buddy Bob banged the seat next to him so hard it broke off. For a time, the seating capacity at Shea was reduced to 57,332, since Bob took the seat he broke off home with him.

I grabbed one of the red, white, and blue pieces of bunting that draped the upper deck and snuck it out under my jacket. That bunting became a decorative bed covering for my last two years of high school.

Years later I had my sons skip school and off to Shea Stadium we went for opening day. I would send a note letting their school know that they needed to attend an 'important' family function.

Early in our relationship I took my wife Norma to a night game at Shea. It was her first major league game. As we walked in, her eyes filled with tears. Her father played baseball in Mexico where she grew up. He was a huge fan and he loved to take her to games when she was a little girl. She'd sit on his lap as he explained the nuances of baseball.

Her dream was to bring her dad to a NY Mets game and maybe the Hall of Fame in Cooperstown, NY. But that was not to be. He passed away before that could happen.

Each year Norma and I fly to a National League city to watch a Mets game. Of course, we also go to the local art museum, eat the local fare, and listen to music. But it is the ballgame that is the primary draw for us.

I have collected signed baseballs of several of my favorite Mets players which I keep in my office. I also have a pair of red upper deck seats in my family room from Shea Stadium which was demolished in 2008 to make way for the Mets new home, CitiField.

A brick in the sidewalk at the main entrance to CitiField proudly states:

Litsky Family
Loyal Mets Fans since 1962

Baseball has been a constant in my life and the life of my family. My grandfather spoke of Hank Greenberg a fellow Jew from the Bronx, who once nearly toppled Babe Ruth's single season home run record.

My father talked of Joltin' Joe DiMaggio and his hitting streak of 56 consecutive games, though he might have been more famous for being married to Marilyn Monroe.

I look back on the days of Mickey Mantle patrolling center field at Yankee Stadium. And my children have their memories of Mookie Wilson and the 1986 World Champion NY Mets.

Sadly, my four grandchildren prefer swimming, hockey, art and music.

There is hope for them yet.

High School baseball team. I am top row on the left.

1

— • —

THE BIG RED KISS

I sat quietly, nervously watching the second hand ever so slowly roll around the wall clock above the black board at the front of our class.

It was the last day of 4th grade at PS 176. Summer for us would begin sharply at 3:00 pm, but first I had to get through the day. It felt like – and indeed it was – the longest day of the year.

June 21st is also my birthday. This was year number nine. And I was terrified. But we'll get to that in a moment.

As with every other school day, it started with the Pledge of Allegiance. I had only recently learned that we were not pledging to the flag and some guy named *Richard Stands.'* The words were, *"for which it stands.'"* Not the first time in my life I would mishear something.

9:00 am. We sat and started on our reading. It was the last day of school.

"If we couldn't read by then, one more hour wasn't going to help."

10:00 am. On to a little math. Fractions. Pies in my house were never cut in equal pieces. I stared out the large window facing the empty asphalt playground where I would soon be spending my summer days.

"How slow does this clock move?"

"Why couldn't I have been born in July or August. I did not want to celebrate my birthday during the school year."

1

12:00 noon. Finally. We were released for lunch. A one-hour dash home. I lived four blocks away on 233rd Street. Just close enough to run home and eat a peanut butter and jelly sandwich (strawberry jam) on white bread cut on a diagonal and get back to school before the bell rang leaving me to stare at the clock as our school year wound down.

My teacher was Mrs. Simonetti. She was a sweet lady who wore the same emerald green dress almost every day. This was complimented by a string of large white pearls (most likely plastic) and large earrings to match.

She was old. Maybe 40.

Her most striking feature was her blood red lipstick. What she was known best for was making her students birthdays '*special.*' Special to her was a nightmare for me.

At the end of the school day, she would have the birthday student come up to the head of the class. All the children would sing '*Happy Birthday.*' And then she'd put the student over her lap. And give the child one loving smack on the ass for each year of his life.

For good luck, she would plant a KISS with those huge red lips on his face. Yuck!!! I wanted no part of this.

2:00 pm. As we began tackling the afternoon lesson, some crap about the Dutch settling in NYC, the clock ticked on ever so slowly.

"*Come on. No one cares. It is summer and time to get the hell out of school.*"

2:45 pm. "*I think I'm going to make it.*"

"*Ok children, close your books and leave them on top of your desk,*" she said. "*Before the last bell of the year rings and your summer begins, we have a birthday boy.*"

Everyone knew what that meant.

She pulled her chair around to the front of her big desk and invited me to stand next to her while my class sang "Happy Birthday."

Over the lap I went. The room, full of who I thought were my friends, counted each whack with increasing frenzy and laughter. And then, just as the final bell rang, she planted a big sloppy, wet red kiss smack on my right cheek.

We lined up and headed for the door. Summer at last!

There was a birthday tradition in those days at PS 176. The boys in the class would take turns punching the birthday boy on the arm. One punch for each year.

That is if they could catch me.

They caught me immediately, and I was vastly outnumbered. The punches came furiously while I was held by the biggest boys in the class.

So I started the summer vacation of my ninth year with bruises on my right arm that didn't fade until the Fourth of July. As much as my arm hurt it did serve to take some of the emotional sting away from that big red kiss.

To this day when I see a woman with bright red lipstick, I remember the big red kiss and I cringe.

I'm the second child in from Mrs. Simonetti.
Note the oversized ears.

2

---・---

A Hot Dog, a Coke and a Fantasy - Two Bucks!

E very neighborhood had a bowling alley. It was open morning to
night, and it was cheap fun. And best of all we could spend a few
hours completely unsupervised.

Ours was Rosedale Lanes on Merrick Boulevard in Laurelton, about a
mile or so from my house in Cambria Heights.

Most Saturday mornings my buddies would meet me at the corner and
bike to Rosedale. We'd lock our bikes together and chain them to the
wrought iron handrail. Although I don't know why anyone would want
to steal these bikes. Ours were on their second or third owners and were
pretty much beat to hell.

Two dollars would pay for the shoe rental, two games, a hot dog and
soda. Occasionally, there would be a little money left over for a slice of pizza
on the way home.

The bowling alley had 24 lanes. Most of them were occupied. To our
left, there was a large sign that simply said "SHOES." Beneath the sign was
Anthony. As always, he wore a tight white T-shirt with a pack of Winston's
rolled up in his left sleeve. He wore extra slim blue jeans to show off his
body. In those days we called them dungarees.

Not a strand of his long, black hair was out of place. Brylcreem Hair Cream. He was constantly combing it with a plastic comb ever present in his back pocket. To us he was the epitome of cool. He was "*the shoe guy.*" Our shoe guy. A few years later he wound up in Vietnam. And we never saw him again.

We were eight years younger and sported crew cuts. A half inch of hair growing straight up on our heads trimmed neatly around the ears. A fresh haircut gave us the appearance of having white wall tires on each side of our noggins.

We would slip off our shoes and slap them down on the counter. All Anthony wanted to know was our shoe sizes. He placed my sneakers in a cubby space and pulled out a multicolored pair advertising to all that I wore a 9 ½ shoe. Once he collected a quarter, gave the shoes a quick spray of awful smelling disinfectant, we were ready to bowl.

The manager assigned us a lane. I don't remember his name, but I do remember the anchor tattoo on his enormous right forearm. Yeah, just like Popeye.

While we waited for our lane to open, we scoured the ball racks for a ball that best fit our three fingers. All the black balls were 16 lbs. The more colorful ones were lighter and for girls or children.

The trophy case always caught my attention. If you were under 13 and bowled a game of 150 you could take home a 12" high plastic trophy. I wanted that golden trophy even more than getting to second base with Marcia, a classmate who recently graduated from her training bra. Thus far my highest score was 110. My score with Marcia was 0.

Finally, our lane opened, and we began our complicated Saturday ritual of choosing sides. It was a combination of *Rock, Paper, Scissors* and *Eenie, Meenie, Miney, Mo.*

The side with the highest combined scores of the two games got to win a DARE. The losing side would have to do something ridiculous or slightly dangerous although in good humor.

For the next hour we bowled, laughed, and teased each other. We took turns keeping score with a stubby little golf pencil on lined paper with tiny boxes. We argued loudly and often. About math. These were the pre-calculator days. And these little pencils had no erasers.

An hour later we were done. Joey and I lost, and no one came close to a score of 150 to claim a trophy. The DARE of the day was that we would have to put a small piece of our hot dog into one of the balls on the rack.

To the snack bar we went. We hopped up on four of the counter stools and waited for Jennifer to take our order. She was a curvaceous high school girl with shoulder length blonde hair. Somehow, she knew her exaggerated movements drove the boys crazy. And it also increased her tips.

Secretly, we admitted to each other that we had fantasies about our waitress being naked. Every twelve-year-old boy is perpetually horny and has a vivid imagination. We were no different.

We ordered four hot dogs and cokes. And spun around on the stools until we got dizzy.

We paid for our snack and left our remaining money on the table as a tip. Joey and I each took about an inch of our hot dogs (his with mustard, mine with ketchup) and walked toward the long rows of bowling balls.

I don't know where or if Joey put his hot dog piece in a ball. He struck me as a guy who would chicken out. I chose a black ball on the lower shelf to deposit my hot dog piece. The thumb hole was huge. I figured anyone with thumbs that big would be too fat to chase us.

As we returned our shoes, I glanced over to see two very large men with fat, meaty hands entering the alley. We hurriedly put on our sneakers, ran out to our bikes, and headed back to the safety of our neighborhood.

We spent the rest of the day laughing about our Saturday outing. On the way home we made a quick stop at the McDonald's, which was brand new to Queens. Even better, we had a couple of neighborhood friends working there who would load up our bags with extra burgers and fries for us to feast on.

I now find myself bowling about once every 10 years. And some things don't ever change. There are always a few obnoxious young teens hanging out which always brings a smile to my face. And I never put my fingers in a bowling ball without first taking a quick peek inside the holes.

I've yet to bowl a game of more than 150. But when I finally do, I'm going to buy myself the cheap plastic bowling trophy I've longed for all these years.

3

— · —

SHE ROLLED HER R'S AND CROSSED HER LEGS

Miss Fagan perched on the edge of her desk. Every so often she would cross her legs. And drive the boys in my 7th grade Spanish class crazy.

She was a new teacher. Fresh out of school. JHS 59 was her first assignment. And she was the prettiest girl/woman I had ever seen outside of a magazine.

Her skirts were mid-thigh. Not quite the mini-skirt length sweeping the fashion world at that time. Nevertheless, it still left nothing to the imagination. And boys in mid-puberty have vivid imaginations.

When class ended, every boy needed a few extra minutes before rising. I had to walk to my next class holding a textbook in front of my pants every time she wore the low-cut red dress.

I blame Miss Fagan's legs on my inability to speak Spanish.

At twelve I could feel the world was changing and so was I.

Civil rights. JFK. The Beatles. The Cold War. Vietnam. The world was spinning.

I was in junior high school. A mouthful of braces, a face full of zits, pigeon-toed with hormones out of control. I was too old to be a kid. Yet too young to be a man.

At 8 am a thousand of us would arrive at the school yard. It felt more like a prison yard, the kind I'd seen in the movies. Most days there was a fight that ramped up the schoolyard cacophony into a fever pitch until it was broken up. The offenders were hauled off to Mr. Effron's office. He was the Dean of Discipline. It was his job to maintain control of too many 7th and 8th graders. And he did a shitty job.

On the fourth day of junior high school an 8th grader named Phillip asked me if he could hold my lunch money. I told him no and was immediately pummeled with his fists.

His hands were incredibly fast. By the time I realized I was in a fight and got my hands up a teacher pulled him off me.

Phillip was headed to Mr. Effron's office. I was told to clean myself up in the boy's room before the bell rang. I hurried along as I didn't want to miss my first period. Spanish class.

The sight of Miss Fagan's legs always made me feel better.

A few months later Phillip took my friend George's money at knife point. That was the last straw. Phillip was gone and never seen again. Smart money had him ending up in prison. I guessed he might end up as the Dean of Discipline at a junior high school someday.

My parents thought it would be a good idea for me to join the school band. They signed me up to play the French Horn. Each time I hit an F sharp, the overhead light in my basement would vibrate until one day I got it to shatter. Thus ended my musical career.

But I had bigger issues. Marcia grew a pair of boobs over the summer. And I wanted to get to second base.

Then the world came to Queens. The 1964 New York World's Fair. This was a very big deal. They loaded up the 7th graders in a bunch of buses for the 20-minute ride over to Flushing. And they let us loose. With no adult supervision.

The fair was simply amazing. Admission for children was a buck.

The pavilions and exhibits were mostly free. And the lines were short.

There were Pavilions from dozens of countries. Most of the states. And a parade of industries from cars to chemicals. Of course, there was food and music everywhere.

Everything was brightly colored, loud and in motion. A monorail system and gondolas moved crowds across the 700-acre fair. Helicopters landed at the heliport. There was a gigantic Ferris Wheel from a tire company.

IBM unveiled its miracle computer, which appeared to be the size of my house. And it could beat you at *Tic-Tac-Toe!* But so could the trained chicken in Chinatown. Now *that* was amazing. I was pretty sure this computer thing would go nowhere.

AT&T unveiled its picture phone of the future. You could make a call to a friend on the other side of the pavilion, and have a face-to-face chat. My only complaint was that the screen was too high off the ground to moon each other. I didn't see much value in this either.

We rode in silence on a moving sidewalk past Michelangelo's 'Pieta' in the Vatican Pavilion. I was too young to appreciate it. When I saw it again decades later it took my breath away.

But the biggest hit of the fair was the Belgian Waffle. Now *that* was a sculpture.

The two-inch-high waffle was fluffy, deep-ridged and the size of a grown man's hand. Covered with whipped cream, fresh strawberries and pow-dered sugar.

It was only a dollar. I ate two for lunch.

What I remember most about the 1964 World's Fair was the NYC exhibit. It was a meticulous scale model of the City of New York. Every building. All five boroughs. Set up in a space about the size of a Walgreens.

You slowly rode around its perimeter in an unlit car. Somehow, I managed to get Marcia into my car.

Alone with her at last. This was my moment. I was going to get to second base. The doors closed. Lights off.

The car moved ever so slowly around Queens. Then up to the Bronx. As we approached Yankee Stadium, I stretched my arm out around her. She rested her head on my shoulder.

I moved my arm a little higher. My hand found its target.

"Gold! I made it. I am on second base. Wow!", I screamed in my head.

But it felt strange. There was a hard bone in the middle of her breast. I didn't know that boobs had bones. I continued to caress her breast until we rolled around the rest of the city.

Finally, back in Queens, the lights came on and the doors slowly opened. I was now a man!

Marcia ran off giggling to find her girlfriends. I could hardly wait to tell my buddy, Richie, what happened.

I described my conquest to him in great detail. But instead of patting me on the back in admiration, he said words that I will never forget.

"Schmuck! You felt up her shoulder. You didn't get to second base. You got picked off first."

We both laughed so hard we nearly fell down.

Walking back to the bus we passed the Spanish Pavilion. It won the award as the Best International Pavilion. Flamenco dancers were putting on a show out front. Beautiful elaborately costumed women moving to syncopated rhythms. Everyone was having fun. Eating. Drinking. And, of course, speaking Spanish.

I made myself a promise.

From that day forward I would pay less attention to Miss Fagan's legs. And more attention to learning Spanish.

I didn't.

4

—·—

WE CALLED HIM STINKY

You know, there once was a time before pooper-scoopers, and responsible dog owners with plastic bags who picked up after their four-legged friends.

We lived a block away from 121st Ave in Cambria Heights. A concrete sidewalk served as a median strip dividing the wide road.

There were no open grassy places to walk a dog in our neighborhood. So 121st Ave served as the community "dog park".

Three times a day owners walked their dogs. And the crap piled up.

My friends and I prided ourselves on our creativity. Our ability to make a game or a competition out of just about anything was legendary.

We played the usual games. Stoopball. Stickball. Kick the can. Until one day we discovered creative ways to use firecrackers.

It was summer. We had time on our hands and no adult supervision. I'm not sure which of us came up with the idea of lighting a firecracker in a pile of dog crap but at age 11 it proved irresistible.

We spent a lovely afternoon exploding the crap along 121st Ave. We had lots of firecrackers and an almost unlimited supply of dog crap to blow up. And then we came up with the ultimate game. *Shit Storm.*

Explode the firecracker in the middle of a pile of dog crap at the precise moment a car drives by – and you were the winner.

I'm not sure where the expression '"Shit Storm" comes from, but we might have been the first to use it.

We estimated that a car traveling at 30 mph would hit our pile of exploding dog crap if the 5-second fuse was lit when the car was 250 feet or half a block away.

We were not great at math. And had not yet had the opportunity of failing algebra. So, this was more of a hit and miss exercise. The game was simple enough. Light the fuse. Yell, *"Shit Storm!"* And take off running.

We agreed to take turns. Call it a "Rite of Passage."

I went first. I lit my fuse. Screamed, *"Shit Storm!"* Ran like hell. The firecracker exploded. But the flying carnage of crap missed the oncoming car by a good 25 yards.

Willie was next. *"Shit Storm!"* we yelled. He got closer to his mark. And his crap went vertical as he placed his firecracker low in the pile of dog crap. But still he couldn't get the timing quite right to hit the oncoming car.

Then it was Jimmy's turn. Let me tell you about Jimmy. In every group there is someone who tries hard. But doesn't quite fit in. Jimmy was always last to be picked when we chose sides for a game.

We liked him. And we kept an eye on him. He was a little younger and a little slower.

And then we saw it. A fast-moving GTO was headed our way at a rapid speed. Jimmy placed his firecracker. And lit the match. He waited an extra second or two to make sure the fuse was lit. Just as he yelled, *"Shit Storm!"*, it blew. And he was covered by a pile of poodle poop.

The GTO safely darted past. Its driver almost lost control of his vehicle. Probably from hilarity.

We ran home as fast as we could. From that day forward we had a story we would tell over and over again - for years. And Jimmy had a new nickname.

Stinky.

5

EDISON WOULD HAVE CRIED

And then there was the time I nearly burnt down my house. I didn't mean to. I blame it on the poor science education I received at PS 176.

One afternoon I watched the movie *Young Tom Edison* on channel 9's *Million Dollar Movie.* I thought it would be a great idea to invent something that would change the world.

If I could harness the energy of lightning my parents would never have to pay another electric bill. And I would get first prize at the school science fair.

It sounded so simple. Time to experiment.

There was a ten-foot metal pole in my parent's garage. It had been there since we moved into the house five or six years earlier. It had no purpose. Until now.

I wrapped wire around the base of the metal pole. I then hoisted it up through the basketball hoop that hung on the front of the garage. Somehow it managed to stay in place supported by ropes, duct tape and luck.

The top of the pole was now almost 20 ft. off the ground well above the roof line of the garage. Then I ran the wire from the pole through the basement window. And connected it to a light fixture. All I needed now was lightning. I didn't have to wait long.

The lightning came in the form of my father coming home from work.

"Are you out of your freaking mind? What the hell is wrong with you?"

I could see the vein on his forehead bulge a bit. He made me dismantle my experiment. Which, looking back, probably would have burnt down my house.

I still don't know anything about harnessing energy. And the world is a safer place without my science experiments.

From that day forward when I hear the expression, *"I wouldn't touch that with a ten-foot pole,"* I think about the day I tried to give my parents free electricity.

My childhood home in Queens.

6

BEING 12

"*Who's Dick Hertz?*" "*Isabelle Wringing?*" "*Anita Mann?*"

Admit it. You smiled. The junior high schooler in you remembers putting a substitute teacher through hell. Writing on the sign-in sheet names like Ben Dover. Or Seymour Butts.

Occasionally, a less experienced substitute would read the sign-in sheet aloud. And we'd guffaw for the remainder of the period. Sometimes all day.

Yes. We were idiots. The only excuse I have is that I was 12, immature, flooded with hormones and struggling to find my own identity.

Meanwhile our world was moving at an ever-increasing speed.

This was the year police dogs and fire hoses were unleashed on protesters in Birmingham. When Civil rights leader Medgar Evers was murdered in Mississippi. When George Wallace stood in the doorway to stall efforts to integrate the University of Alabama.

And it was the year of Martin Luther King's *I Have a Dream* speech.

A year earlier, the Russian missiles in Cuba nearly set the world on fire. President Kennedy was then shot down in Dallas. And a little place we never heard of called Vietnam would soon create an upheaval our nation had not seen since the Civil War.

But I was 12. I had no voice and no ability to express my thoughts or emotions. No longer a child, I was many years shy of calling myself a man.

It was then that I got hit with a double-barreled punch to the gut.

My classmate Henry Ornstein was murdered. It was the lead story in the newspapers. Big headlines. Above the fold. His body was found in a Greenwich Village apartment. The details were sketchy but our imaginations went wild.

How he ended up an hour and a half away from home in the middle of the night was never explained.

He was the first person I knew who died. My great grandfather and both of my grandparents were still in good health. They would live for many more years.

However, my 12-year-old friend, Henry, would never see another day. In the wink of an eye there was an empty seat in each of my junior high school classes.

The school did nothing to help us deal emotionally with this tragedy. My parents asked only once how I was doing. I could have used a hug but I didn't know how to ask for one.

I just shrugged my shoulders and said I was fine. In those days no one knew how to talk about a dead 12-year-old. So, Henry's memory just faded. Time moved on. And we all graduated into a million different directions.

Much too regularly now, I see news reports of school shootings. A tragedy which thus far has found no solution. Each time I hear of a young person's death the pain of losing Henry bubbles to the surface. And my eyes well up a bit.

Just as we never forget our first kiss. Or our first love. We never forget the first friend who dies.

It has been nearly sixty years since that loss. I can still see his boyish face, the crazy twinkle in his eye and hear his contagious hyena-like laugh. How I could have used a friend like Henry to help me navigate the tumultuous 60's and my eventual entry into adulthood.

It would be Henry who would write Dick Hertz, Yuri Nate and Phil McGroin on the substitute's sign-in sheet. I don't miss being a 12-year-old. But I still miss Henry.

7

ME AND THE MICK

It broke my heart when he fell off the pedestal on which I placed him.

The story began such a long time ago.

I was sitting on the front stoop. A group of neighborhood boys walked up and asked if I was the *"New Kid."* We had just moved to Queens from the Bronx. My parents were unpacking inside the house. My older brother Andy was more social than me. He was already out making new friends. I was five.

"Yeah, I guess I am. We just moved in. I'm Eric," I managed to stammer out.

Then they asked the deep and profound philosophical question of the day.

"Are you a Giant, a Dodger or a Yankee?"

The year was 1956, the last year NYC had three major league baseball teams. The Giants and Dodgers would soon depart to California.

I had no idea what they were talking about. So, I took a shot.

"I'm a Giant."

I figured that was the biggest, though not sure of what. So, they pushed me down on the concrete sidewalk.

"Wrong answer, ass face. Wanna try again?"

I was close to tears, but I kept it together enough to ask what they were.

"We're Yankees," they said almost in unison.

"So am I. I'm Yankees, too."

That seemed to satisfy them. Though I still had no idea what we were talking about. I just didn't want to get pushed down again.

So, I became a Yankee. And over that first summer in my new home, I learned that my new God was a guy named Mickey. Not the mouse. The ballplayer. Mickey Mantle, the Yankees spectacular centerfielder.

This was the year that he won the Triple Crown, leading the major leagues in batting average, home runs and runs batted in -- rare feat which has happened only four times in my lifetime.

Mickey was the brightest star of the best team in baseball. He was the toast of New York. Every boy wanted to be him. And, I can only assume, every woman wanted to take him home.

It was Mickey Mantle who hit a home run for my 10th birthday at the first game I would ever attend at Yankee Stadium.

Thirty years later while working at an advertising agency in Connecticut I hired the long-retired Hall of Fame player to sign autographs at the opening of a bank branch. The bank was our largest client, and the bank president loved the Yankees.

Mickey spent the afternoon signing baseballs and having his photo taken with anyone who opened a new account. He looked like he hated every minute of it.

When his four-hour stint was up, he said, *"I'm thirsty. Let's go find a bar."*

A half hour later our entourage of eight was at a neighborhood bar in Waterbury.

It was there that my childhood idol fell off the pedestal I had placed him on so many years earlier.

I tried to match my one lite beer to every two double vodkas he consumed but I couldn't keep up. The more he drank the more I got concerned about his health. A liver could only handle so much. Some years later he needed a new liver.

More shocking to me was the language he used describing players of color. Though he spent his career as a New York superstar athlete, he was still a small-town Southern boy with a vocabulary peppered with inappropriate racial slurs.

In front of me was a man who could bring 60,000 people to their feet with the swing of his bat. But on this day, he was a tired old man who drank entirely too much. And became handsy with some of the women.

Mickey Mantle died a dozen years later from a variety of medical complications exacerbated by his consumption of alcohol.

But at age five he was my hero. My first hero.

I'm the one with the mustache next to my childhood hero.

8

MAX AND NAT

They nearly killed my brother.

My uncles Max and Nat could fix almost anything. They worked out of a small shop in the basement of Max's Brooklyn house. Their puttering and tinkering supplemented their living. Both were high school shop teachers.

Max drove an old Volvo. A Volvo today in the Prospect Park section of Brooklyn would be a pretty typical ride. This part of Brooklyn is now full of wealthy Manhattan ex-pats. Here you can buy a house with a back yard and a tree in front. A nice place to raise a family, rather than being jammed into a small Manhattan apartment.

Volvos today are not cheap.

But this was not today. It was the mid 1960s. Max's old Volvo was falling apart as was much of the surrounding neighborhood. A Volvo back then was more than unusual. It was rare. So too was finding parts. Finding a mechanic who knew how to fix it was nearly impossible.

This didn't bother Max. If he and Nat couldn't find a part, they would simply make one in their basement shop.

One afternoon they were babysitting for my little brother, Tom, while my parents went to a Broadway matinee. Tom was a bright and curious six-year-old who enjoyed watching them tinker. Max and Nat would put Tom to work. Sweeping the floor, separating miscellaneous screws and bolts. All the things a six-year-old could do and feel like a part of the team.

Max's basement looked like a hardware store stocked full of all kinds of tools Tom had never seen. My dad owned a hammer which he used mainly to hang pictures. He had a handsaw which I never saw him use and his screwdriver was a butter knife which may have had a bit of crusty cream cheese lodged in the serrated edge. He was not a handy man. We lived in a house of not very handy men. I still do.

On this day the work project was automotive. Max's muffler was shot. You could hear him coming from a half a block away. Since there was no place in Brooklyn to pick up a new Volvo muffler at a reasonable price, Max and Nat decided to repair it. How hard could that be?

Tom watched as they jacked up the Volvo on the street in front of the house. They removed the old muffler. The three of them stared at it for some time. Tom had an urge to tell them to take it to "the guy." Most households in those days had a 'fix it' guy to call. To fix stuff. He was generally referred to simply as "the guy."

But Max and Nat *were* the "guys" who got the calls to fix stuff. Even though they had never seen a Volvo muffler before, they determined that the piping from the muffler needed to be repaired.

So, they soldered an empty can of Del Monte cling peaches to a couple of A&P tuna fish cans that they pulled from the trash and inserted it back into the muffler. That seemed to work.

The muffler was then reconnected to the underside of the Volvo.

Voila! They had themselves a repaired muffler. Total cost: about a buck and a half. And they had cling peaches left over for a lunchtime snack.

Max started up the Volvo while Nat leaned in the open car window offering encouraging words to his brother.

The car started up and was humming like it just rolled off the showroom floor. For the first time in weeks, you could have a normal conversation standing next to the running engine. The muffler was deemed successfully repaired. As they were enjoying the quiet and a few moments of self-congratulation, the engine heated up the now reattached muffler.

It didn't take long for the heat to cause the soldering job to come loose. And then with no warning one of the tin cans they soldered shot out from the underbelly of the Volvo like a Civil War cannon.

The can embedded itself deep in the maple tree my brother Tom was standing next to. Six inches to the right and there would have been a tuna can sized hole in my little brother. That would have been tough to explain to my parents.

Tom survived. The tree survived. And the old Volvo ran for many more Brooklyn miles with an interesting array of replacement parts.

My uncles were delightful guys whose company I thoroughly enjoyed. Even though they nearly killed my little brother on a sunny afternoon in Brooklyn.

9

STAMP THIS

When I was a kid the most printed words in the English language were "close cover before striking." They were on every book of matches. And there were matchbooks everywhere.

I used to like to play with matches. That is until I burnt the tip of my thumb and index finger. And almost set fire to my house.

On the inside of each matchbook was an ad. The particular ad that caught my attention was from The Jamestown Stamp Company of Jamestown, NY.

I was simply impressed that they named the city after the Stamp Company. Or so I thought. Their ad offered a bag of foreign stamps for free. And they would then send *'stamps on approval'* each month.

I had recently been given my dad's old stamp collection. I spent hours carefully removing stamps from his old book into the sleek new stamp album I got for my 11th birthday.

All I had to do was fill out the form on the matchbook and mail it off to them. And I would dramatically increase the size of my collection.

In addition to my address, it asked for my age. I scribbled in 11 which looked like 21.

About a month later there was an oversized envelope from The Jamestown Stamp Company along with a formal letter welcoming me. It was the first official letter I ever received addressing me as Mr. Litsky. Pretty cool for an 11-year-old. It had a lot of information about how their 'on approval' system worked. I didn't understand any of it. So I threw it out.

These stamps were from all over the world. The African stamps were the largest and the prettiest. A lot of those countries were brand new, having recently become independent from the European countries that had colonized them. As an unsophisticated 11-year-old, I guessed that pretty stamps were their way of advertising.

A month later another package came from The Jamestown Stamp Company. Wow. More stamps in dozens of 2 inch, see-through envelopes. I placed them into my album using tiny transparent mounting hinges, with a pair of tweezers I took from my parent's bathroom.

Another month passed and lo and behold there was yet another package from The Jamestown Stamp Company. Along with that month's stamps was a note reminding me to either return the stamps or forward a check in the amount of $12.37.

Since the stamps were already in my album. And I didn't have a checkbook, or for that matter $12.37, I threw the letter away.

And the stamps kept coming.

One October afternoon I came home from school to find a letter with an embossed return address. It was made out to me. It was from a collection agency. I knew I was in trouble.

When my dad came home, I showed him the letter. I was terrified at what his reaction would be. One of two things would happen.

One – he would yell at me for a while and make me send the stamps back.

Or Two – he would yell at me for a while and send me to my room for a month.

What I hadn't considered was a third option. He quietly read the letter. His face squinched up a bit and turned a shade of pinkish red. The vein in his forehead bulged out. I thought he was either going to have a stroke or reach out and kill me dead.

He started to shake. His shoulders moved up and down. His head was in his hands.

And then it started. He burst out in an explosion of laughter. I had never seen my dad laugh like this before. And I didn't know what to do. So, I laughed along with him, for no reason other than to break the tension I was feeling. Unbeknownst to me, that would be the heartiest laughter we ever shared together.

After a few minutes he caught his breath and told me what was so damned funny.

When he was a boy about my age, he started the very stamp collection I now had after responding to the offer of free stamps from The Jamestown Stamp Company. And he, too, received a few packages of stamps "on approval" but never paid for them. When he received a letter from the collection agency, he also tossed it away.

My father was a NYC policeman. Not a man easily intimidated. He said I shouldn't worry about the collections people. I was underage and I would not be going to prison. Phew!

He said he would call and straighten it out. And he hoped someday I would find a way to make it right.

And so, some 60 years later, I did.

Eric V. Litsky
Simsbury, CT 06070

December 5, 2022

Jamestown Stamp Company, Inc
117 Cheney Street
Jamestown, NY 14701-3810

Dear Jamestown Stamp Company:

Sometime in the 1960s as an 11-year-old boy I ordered stamps 'on approval' from your company. After numerous attempts to collect what I owed you, you were informed that I was a minor and I never heard from you again.

I assure you I was not trying to steal your stamps. I just didn't know what 'on approval' meant. I was not the brightest stamp in the album.

The stamps you sent me were placed in the collection my father had when he was a child. As it turns out his collection was comprised of stamps he was sent on approval. Also from The Jamestown Stamp Company.

You didn't collect any money from him either.

Time to correct my inadvertent error.

Please find enclosed a check in the amount of $12.37. Additionally, I still have the stamp collection started by my father thanks to you. If you'd like I would be happy to return the entire album since neither of us paid for the stamps.

My only request is that you pay the postage.

Sincerely yours,
Eric Litsky
Former Philatelist

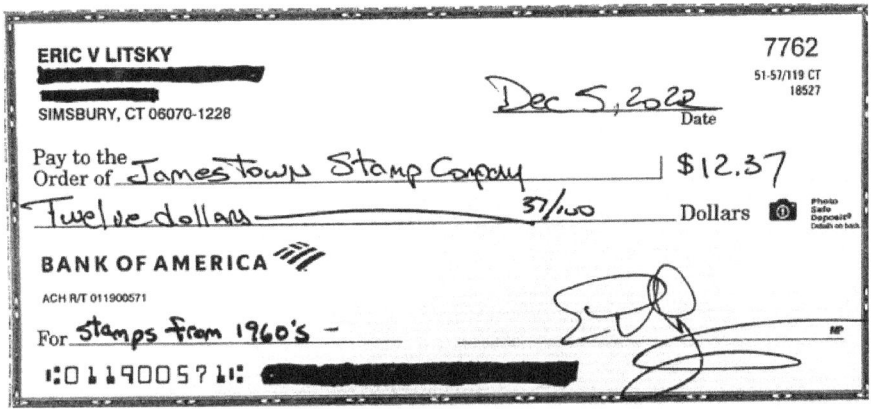

They cashed the check and never wrote back.

10

REPAIR THE WORLD

The smoke from a burnt-out car a block away filled the air. We were used to bad air. Our apartment was just across from the Bethlehem Steel plant. Pollutants of all kinds belched out from dozens of smokestacks each day.

Nevertheless, a nearby overturned car on fire gave us reason to pause.

This was the summer of 1967. We arrived in Lackawanna, NY the same week 2,000 army paratroopers arrived in Detroit to patrol the streets in tanks and armored carriers in order to quell the rioting there.

Lackawana is a four-hour drive from Detroit. It was about as far as you could get from the *'Summer of Love'* being celebrated by 100,000 hippies in the Haight-Ashbury section of San Francisco. A part of me wanted to be there.

Instead, I spent that sweltering summer with the AJSS (American Jewish Society for Service) as a volunteer with a group of teens making repairs to a deteriorating garden apartment complex.

Sixteen of us lived in a few empty apartments there. We were pretty much the only white faces in the area; working in our small way to repair the world.

The concept of social action to improve the world runs deep in the Jewish tradition. In Hebrew it is called *"Tikkun olam."* In English, *"Repair the world."*

Over time the neighbors came to appreciate our efforts as we fixed broken windows, torn screens and cement walks.

After work, I would sit on the apartment's stoop drinking a cold soda. In that part of the country, they call it pop. One afternoon a couple of little girls came by and asked if they could touch my hair. It had grown quite long. They had never seen a white boy up close and were curious about my hair.

"Sure," I said.

Twenty minutes later six of them were putting my hair in cornrows. It hurt like hell. But there was a lot of laughter. And I looked ridiculous. Our neighbors watched from their windows. Smiling at the happy commotion.

After a time, we became less of an oddity and more a part of the texture of this small community.

Though there was rioting in dozens of African American communities that summer including nearby Buffalo, things here in Lackawana were pretty calm. We were referred to as *"blue-eyed soul brothers."* Although I'm not sure if any of us actually had blue eyes.

I had the sense that if the shit really hit the fan here, our neighbors would offer us some level of protection.

One afternoon a young boy came by on his bicycle and mumbled something which sounded like, *"Could you be my brother?"*

I was deeply honored and humbly said, *"Of course."*

I didn't realize what he actually said was, *"Could you BEAT my brother?"*

35

A day or so later his brother came by looking to kick my ass. He was bigger than me and quite muscular. I had to think fast or get a serious beat down.

Once I understood that I misheard the younger boy I told him I thought his brother meant *"beat me at basketball."* And so, the game was on. We played one on one. Street rules. No fouls were called. For the next 20 minutes we battered each other.

He was faster than I was. But he couldn't stop my jump shot. In the end he won a hard-fought game. I bought us cold pops. Though I had some bruises, it was better than the ass whooping he had planned to give me.

I'd like to say we became friends. We never did. But when we saw each other there was a nod of mutual respect.

Perhaps years later he would remember the Jewish teens who lived in his neighborhood during the sweltering summer the Ghettos erupted.

I sure do.

Tikkun Olam

11

— · —

THE LIFEBOAT

Our ship went down. Leaving seven of us in a lifeboat designed for six. We would not be picked up for many days. If we did not reduce our number from seven to six in the next twenty minutes our lifeboat would sink. We would all perish.

No. We couldn't take turns hanging on to the side of the lifeboat. Or, for that matter, swimming next to it. There was no way out. We had to choose as a group - who would be saved and who would perish?

This was a classroom exercise. We were physically safe sitting in a circle on a carpeted floor in a dimly lit room. But the next twenty minutes were going to be traumatic. We were in an emotional pressure cooker.

We wasted five precious minutes bargaining with the professor, trying to find an alternative ending to this dilemma. The set up was organized in such a way that we were left with only one decision to make. We had to lose one of our classmates, or we would all drown.

Welcome to my upper-level class in Interpersonal Communications. I wanted to say, *'fuck you'* and just stand up and walk out. But I needed the grade. I was running a 4.0 in my major: Communications. Accountants and biology majors don't have to deal with this crap.

Discussion ensued.

Around the lifeboat we went. Each of us took a couple of minutes to say why we should be the ones to live. *I'm getting married. I'm a virgin. I've never traveled. I've never fallen in love.* About what you'd expect.

Each minute we were reminded that the clock was ticking down. And with each ensuing minute the anxiety in our group rose accordingly.

Then they finally got around to me to beg for my life.

"Are we to act like this is a real situation?" I asked.

The answer was that I had a little more than two minutes, or we would all drown.

With that, I gently pushed the girl next to me out of the boat.

She burst out in tears. And for the rest of the class everyone tore into me like I was some kind of mad killer.

"You're an animal. Machiavelli. How could you do this to her?"

I thought they might thank me for making such a tough decision, and for saving all of our lives.

Our professor said she had done this exercise dozens of times. And never had that happened.

Their reactions bothered me all these years. I think this is a horrible exercise which creates a fever pitch of anxiety. If its purpose is to have participants express why they value their lives, surely there are better ways to accomplish that goal.

The young woman I pushed out of the boat approached me weeks later.

"Why did you choose to push me out of the boat?" she asked with teary eyes.

"You were to my right and I only had a few seconds left. It wasn't about you. I am right-handed. And I am truly sorry."

So, my gentle reader, be honest. If this were a real situation, what would you have done?

12

The Peanut Farmer

He was a peanut farmer who also happened to be the Governor of Georgia.

I was a young advertising guy a year out of college.

We were both largely unknown outside of our immediate circles. A short time later Jimmy Carter became very well known. Our nation's 39th President.

I, on the other hand, continue to live in relative obscurity.

The year was 1976. Each of the original 13 states organized a Bicentennial Commission to celebrate our nation's 200th anniversary. The funding source was the sale of each state's Bicentennial Commemorative Coins. The company which produced these coins was a client of the advertising agency where I worked.

Our task was to produce radio and television commercials for each state featuring its Governors.

I flew to Atlanta with Mike from our office. He was a couple of years older than me. We were the young guys in the agency. The commercials for the other 12 states had already been completed. Frankly, no one else wanted to go to Georgia. So off we went.

But this story is not about Jimmy Carter. Atlanta. Or the Bicentennial. It is about two clueless kids on their first business trip.

For the record, Jimmy Carter took a couple of minutes to read the script. The camera rolled. He did it in one take.

For the rest of my years in advertising, I never experienced anyone memorizing a script so quickly, and then nailing it in one take. I thought, "*This is one smart guy.*"

We were in and out of his office in about a half hour. With a half day of free time on our hands before we had to fly home.

These were the days when Atlanta had not yet risen to become a great American city. It still had a very small-town feel.

In a tourist trap called 'Underground Atlanta' the racist former governor of Georgia, Lester Maddox, had a gift shop. He sold white t-shirts with red necks. Cute idea. And he also autographed ax handles. They were a symbol of his defiant resistance to integration. This was not cute. It was disgusting.

Maddox served fourteen years as Governor. Largely forgotten was that he also served four years as Jimmy Carter's Lieutenant Governor.

Mike said, "*Let's grab a cab and go to a strip club out near the airport. We can leave our stuff in the trunk. And have the cab come back for us in time to make our flight.*"

I had never been to Atlanta. Never been on a business trip. And I had never been to a strip club.

"*Sure, why not?*"

We pulled up to a place that advertised in large red blinking neon letters, *Lunch with a View.* We put our stuff in the trunk of the cab and asked him to come back for us in 3 hours.

As we entered the strip club, I realized that my wallet was in the inside pocket of my suit jacket that was now in the trunk of our cab. Which had just pulled out of the parking lot.

There were a lot of things that should have occurred to me. My wallet with my money, driver's license, credit card and my ticket home is being driven in the trunk of a cab which may or may not come back for me.

But I was 23 years old and in the middle of a room full of boobs. Very far from home.

And I am so easily distracted.

Mike said he'd cover lunch and drinks and I could pay him back later. So, we took seats at the bar and washed our fried chicken lunch down with a few too many beers.

"You boys sure like the Governor's peanuts," the half-naked bar maid said as she refilled our bowls from a large bag behind the counter. I glanced down and saw the label.

CARTER'S PEANUTS

For a moment I thought Mike was going to tell the barmaid that we just came from the Governor's office. Mercifully, he did not.

At the appointed hour Mike and I stumbled out of the strip club. Our cab was waiting as promised. We tipped him generously and headed home.

Over the years I've often thought about that day. And how so many things could have gone so very badly.

I guess there is some truth to the expression that, *"God watches out for idiots and drunks."* On that day we were both.

I'm still not a strip club guy. And I rarely drink beer. But I've always had a warm spot in my heart for Jimmy Carter. And, of course, for peanuts.

13

— ◆ —

BIKING THROUGH THE CITY

M y ass hurt and I was exhausted. But it was the best day I had riding since the training wheels came off my bike.

Bike New York sponsors a bicycle tour through the city's five boroughs. The daylong 48-mile ride winds through each borough, over several bridges, and through numerous neighborhoods.

The charity ride brought out more than 30,000 riders the year that I entered with my brother, Tom.

There is no better way to traverse the city than by bike. Through closed streets and thoroughfares. It is a unique way to experience the beauty and diversity of The Big Apple.

Riders are encouraged to take their time and soak in the atmosphere. This is an extraordinary event. It is NOT a race. It is a ride.

Up through the canyons of skyscrapers on 6th Ave. Through Central Park to Harlem. Up to the Bronx where I was born. We slid through some neighborhoods in Queens and Brooklyn. And then back to Manhattan to ride along the East River.

The experience of riding down the FDR Drive on a bike is hard to describe. Two lanes were closed off. So, it was perfectly safe. A lot safer than driving on the Manhattan highway during normal business hours. To me that is always a white-knuckle drive. Dodging potholes and taxis. But biking it was a joy.

So much to see on this peaceful afternoon. It was the first time I could appreciate the beautiful architecture, and the views of the river. It is an entirely different perspective.

Suddenly, several riders screamed by us racing ahead. They looked annoyed at our lackadaisical riding.

Admittedly, I am built for distance, not for speed, and we were riding slowly. I shouted something inappropriate at them as they sped ahead. They were out of earshot before my sentence was out. Much to the delight of the riders next to us.

Their choice was to ride as fast as they could with their heads down. Focusing their attention on their front tires as they hit the road. A pothole at a fast speed can be treacherous. They rode with no appreciation of all that was around them.

My personal highlight was riding over the Verrazzano Bridge back to Staten Island where 8 hours earlier our ride began. The Verrazzano is the longest suspension bridge in the U.S. And this was my first time on it. Until then, my visits to Staten Island, the smallest of the city's five boroughs, had always been on the iconic Staten Island Ferry.

Fun fact. The bridge was named to honor the 16th century Italian explorer, Giovanni da Verrazzano. Originally it was spelled with only one Z. But a battle of orthographers (spelling geeks) resulted in the NY State Legislature adding the second Z. Some fifty years after the bridge was opened.

Who says government doesn't work?

Two things became immediately apparent. First, the bridge is huge rising more than 200 feet above the water. And second, the entrance ramp was not designed for bicycles. It is a very steep ride. Particularly after biking all day through the other four boroughs.

Yet once on the top level the views are remarkable. With lower Manhattan and the flats of Brooklyn in clear view. I marveled at the architectural simplicity and massive size of the Twin Towers which dwarfed everything else in the financial district. It was to be the last time I would see The Towers. On a quiet September morning five months later, they were destroyed. And the world changed forever.

With my brother Tom on our Bike NY ride. The Twin Towers would be destroyed a few months later.

14

THE FARMER IN THE DELL

The company president was running late, and I was getting anxious.

I was in the conference room of a large manufacturing company in Minneapolis. My company was consulting on a project. I was there to deliver our preliminary findings.

I promised my son, Jason, that I would get home in time to hear his concert. So long as I made my flight, I would be able to keep that pledge. I was not sure how important it was to him for me to be there. But it was important to me.

Growing up in a household where my parents rarely attended my events, it was important to me to be there for my kids. Every practice. Every game. Every performance.

This was the spring concert of the Squadron Line Elementary School orchestra. With 10-year-old musicians, I was virtually certain it would be horrible. But I've always believed that successful parenting is mostly about just showing up.

The company president finally stormed into the conference room almost an hour late. There was the usual introductory chatter. He seemed like a genuinely nice guy. Also, the first billionaire I ever met.

I started to go through my presentation rapidly. I was determined to make that plane. Halfway through he, held up his hand.

"Whoa, what's your hurry young man? You got a plane to catch?"

"Well sir, actually, I do. My son has a concert tonight. His first. He is a violinist."

He then shared that he played the violin when he was a boy. And he asked what the program was. I told him I didn't know.

"I tell you what. Get through the material you brought. And I'll have my driver bring the car around to the front door. He'll get you to the airport faster than waiting for a cab."

With that I summarized our initial assessment over the next 20 minutes. And he wished me and my family well on the concert.

"You must be such a proud father."

I was on the elevator and in the back seat of a Lincoln Town Car in about two minutes flat.

"You must have really impressed him. I rarely drive anyone else but him in his car."

"Your boss listens to classical music, doesn't he?"

"It's the only music he likes"

Fifteen minutes later I was running through the airport. I was the last to board.

Back in Hartford, I ran off the plane and to my car which I had left in the short-term lot close to the terminal door.

Twenty minutes later I walked into the elementary school just as the conductor raised her baton. For the next half hour my ears were subjected to a raucous cacophony of screechy violins and squeaky woodwinds. All slightly out of tune. The first number was a somewhat recognizable *The Farmer in The Dell.*

I smiled broadly. Not so much as the proud parent I was, but at the company president. He would be having dinner at this very moment in his gigantic home sharing with his wife how he helped a young man get to his plane in order to hear his son's very first violin concert.

Hi-ho, the derry-o.

15

TREADING WATER

I recently asked a retired guy at a dinner party what he had done in his career.

He went on to recount his work résumé in an amazing amount of detail. Where he went to school. His grades. Why he changed majors. Where he interviewed for his first job and who finally hired him. Then the new title of each promotion and the specifics of what he did.

This detailed recitation went on and on through each of the five jobs he held in his career. I'm not saying a man should not be proud of his work. Just don't take 35 minutes to tell me about it. I think had I not been seated I might have passed out from sheer boredom.

That said, I trust recounting a bit of my work life will entertain you. And not put you into a coma.

After a very brief time as a corporate headhunter (executive recruiter) in NYC, my wife of six months gave me an ultimatum. She hated living there and was going back to Hartford from where we had just relocated. We had taken our newly minted college diplomas to NYC seeking fame and fortune. We found neither. I was free to come with her or stay. Either way she was out.

It's not like I was setting the world on fire. I was also unhappy earning $80 per week as a draw against all the commissions I was promised. Not the first time in my career I was lied to.

I had just turned 22 and found myself riding the Long Island Railroad into the city each day from Great Neck - along with a trainload of lawyers and business executives reading their Wall Street Journals. On the other hand, I was just finishing up Karl Marx's *Das Capital*. This just wasn't a good fit. I was completely out of my element. So, back to Hartford we went, with a total of $600 in our pockets feeling properly deflated.

This was the early 1970's. We had graduated into a recession. A new word for me. It meant, *"Good luck finding a fucking job."* My major was Communications which meant I was qualified to flip burgers or do manual labor. Nothing wrong with either of those jobs, but I had just invested four years of my sweat and treasure to fulfill my dream. I wanted to work in an advertising agency.

These were the days before the personal computer. No LinkedIn, either. So, I job hunted the old-fashioned way. I knocked on doors. I cold called. And I mailed out dozens and dozens of résumés.

Just when I was about to give up, a partner in one of the largest public relations and advertising agencies in the state asked me in for an interview. They were looking for an *"intern to groom,"* which sounded to me like they wanted to cut a young doctor's hair. But I gladly took the interview and was on my very best behavior.

I was hired on a six-month trial basis at $7,500 per year. At first it sounded like a fortune. That is until I did the math. How in the hell can we live on $144.23 (before taxes) per week? But everyone must start somewhere. And unless you are a member of the "Lucky Sperm Club" that start is usually at the bottom.

I arrived early on my first day sporting a new haircut and the tie I wore to weddings. The partner who hired me asked me to take a seat in reception saying that he'd have an office for me shortly.

About 20 minutes later a young woman about my age holding a box of her personal belongings walked past me toward the main entrance. She stopped, turned to me, and burst out crying as she hurriedly exited the offices.

The hiring partner then called out to me and said, "*Your office is now ready.*" As you can imagine, this was a horrible way to start a new job and my new career. Since the job was on a trial basis, I became enormously anxious fearing I'd be the next one carrying out a box of my belongings.

But at least for now I was on the right side of the door. I was the youngest person in the agency by a decade trying to find a place to fit in. My big break came in an interesting way.

An industrial client had a problem. They discovered that the airplane propeller deicer they manufactured could also be used as a waterbed heater. Who knew? The only trouble was that the white shirt/crew-cut engineering types had trouble communicating with the former hippies who comprised most of the waterbed industry.

Enter me.

The waterbed business was booming and at the time my client was the most established entity in the industry. It had credibility. More importantly, it had cash.

They flew me out to California. Until then I had only been as far west as Buffalo. My task was to learn the business and figure out how to engage in this new industry. What I did was smoke a lot of pot with my new waterbed friends. They needed me and my straight-laced client as much as my client needed them.

Within a year I signed up a portfolio of waterbed related accounts including two of the country's largest manufacturers, a chain of waterbed stores and the Los Angeles-based Waterbed Manufacturers Association. To ensure that this new business would stay in the agency they made me a VP and cranked up my salary. Just in time as we now had two babies and a new house mortgaged to the hilt.

In the years that followed, I handled the advertising and public relations for a wide range of clients selling everything from fried chicken to financial services. I have a short attention span so frequently jumping from business to business suited me fine.

I particularly liked working with services or products which were new to the market.

Such was the case with Hartford Jai-Alai.

When Jai-Alai came to Connecticut they hired our agency to explain it to the media and introduce it to the public. The short explanation of the game of Jai-Alai is that it is a competitive sport, and you can bet on it. Remember, this was 50 years or so before Draft Kings. Anyway, it is like handball played on three walls and it is fast-moving and exciting. It had been played in Florida for decades, but staid and conservative Hartford is a long way from the Sunshine State in almost every way possible.

Jai-Alai originated from the Basque region of Spain where it was played against the exterior of cathedral walls. Today the game is played on a court.

Walls are made of granite. And the ball, called a *pelota*, is slightly smaller than a baseball but as hard as a golf ball. The pelota is caught and thrown against the front wall from a scooped wicker basket, called a *cesta*. And it can travel at speeds up to 180 miles per hour. Yes, 180 mph. That is not a typo. It is freaking fast.

Like handball, you've got to catch the ball on no more than one bounce and return it to the front wall, all in one fluid motion.

They sent me to Florida to learn the intricacies of the game. I got to strap on a cesta (sounds like something from a bad porno movie) and tried to catch and throw the pelota. I was a catcher in high school and was used to a baseball coming at me at a high rate of speed. But this was quite another animal.

A good high school pitcher can throw a baseball around 80 mph. I'd catch it in my thick catcher's mitt, protected by shin guards, a mask, a chest protector and a hard plastic cup for the family jewels.

But when I found myself on the court with nothing but my curved wicker cesta strapped to my arm, I was terrified. The players took it easy on me. The rock-hard pelota screamed off from the granite wall at about 125 mph. As I ran off the court the players laughed at me and yelled something in Basque that sounded like *"pelota txikia."* A loose translation I was told was, "little balls."

I spent a year promoting the hell out of the sport and when the fronton (Jai-Alai arena) finally opened, in Hartford, it was to large crowds. Once established, my work with Jai-Alai was basically done. But there is more to this story.

Like all pari-mutuel wagering (horse, dog tracks, etc.) the house takes its cut on every dollar wagered. It was a heady time in the world of Jai-Alai. Money was pouring in hand over fist. It attracted the attention of big money investors and, to no surprise, organized crime. More specifically Boston's notorious Winter Hill Gang which was run by one of the scariest mobsters in New England, Whitey Bolger.

Due to the speed and odd angles the pelota careens off the front court wall as well as the game structure of round robin play, it was said that the game was nearly impossible to fix. *Nearly* being the operative word.

One player couldn't fix a match. But a handful could. And they did. A scandal ensued leaving Jai-Alai with a black eye. Jai-Alai hired more former FBI agents in hopes of cleaning up their image and the game. Unfortunately, several former agents were soon corrupted and ended up behind bars -- or worse.

The business was sold to an investor from Tulsa who soon after ended up murdered. Shortly thereafter, World Jai-Alai's president and a former FBI agent, John Callahan, was found bullet ridden in the trunk of his car at the Miami airport.

But what finally put an end to Hartford Jai-Alai was not the cheating scandals, corrupt former FBI agents or gangland murders. It was a couple of small Connecticut Indian tribes which eventually built the world-class casinos of Foxwoods and Mohegan Sun.

16

---•---

SWIMMING WITH SHARKS

After nearly a decade in the advertising/public relations business, I longed for a new challenge.

One of my clients was a large shopping center developer in need of a full-time marketing director. A year later, my expanded duties included leasing spaces in their shopping centers.

It was on the job training for me. I went to school at night to get my broker's license and I was off to the races. Putting deals together came fairly easy to me once I understood the new vocabulary and how the numbers worked.

My background in marketing was extremely helpful, particularly with local tenants. It was second nature for me to help them with their marketing programs. These 'mom and pop' tenants generally couldn't afford to hire an ad agency. But they got me for free to guide them on how best to market their business in the space they were about to lease.

Many were recent immigrants often with very little command of the English language. I soon discovered that most commercial real estate brokers in my area rarely paid attention to a prospective tenant with a heavy accent. Though it sometimes was a little extra work, I preferred dealing with new arrivals to America.

My grandparents were immigrants who spoke no English when they arrived at Ellis Island. Surely, they received help and guidance from more established Americans back in their day. So, I looked at my work as *paying it forward*. I made new friends from all corners of the globe. Scores and scores of new Americans were soon opening family businesses. I took great joy in that. On more than a few occasions a school-aged child would translate for non-English speaking parents as we worked through the details of complicated commercial leases. They appreciated my honesty and kindness. And I was rewarded.

My clientele expanded and was loyal. They would come back to me for their second or third shop or restaurant. Over the years they would send their friends and other family members. It was great fun for me, and I made a good living.

Then I got a little greedy.

A fast-growing real estate company offered me a huge increase in pay to help them lease the commercial buildings they purchased. It was a big job with a very high-profile firm.

This group sold limited partnership interests in each of the dozens of multi-family and commercial properties they purchased. The three partners lived the life of the rich and famous as millions of dollars flew into their coffers from investors who should have known better.

They treated themselves with Rolls Royce motor cars and large second and third homes. One of the partners built himself a 44,000-sf house featuring 17 bedrooms, 33 bathrooms, a disco, an indoor shooting range, glass elevator, movie theater and, of course, a custom-built waterfall in the backyard. At the time, it was considered the largest single-family residence in the state.

That house later was sold to heavyweight boxer Mike Tyson and then some years later to Rapper 50 Cent. Each made its own improvements to this real estate monstrosity.

The only trouble was that this massive house was built with other people's money. He and his partners ran a full-scale Ponzi scheme that bilked 7,000 people out of their savings. One of their investors was the "very stable genius" himself, Donald Trump.

Their parties were legendary with a guest list that regularly included senators, congressmen and the governor.

But then, as with all Ponzi schemes, it was over in a flash. When the business came crashing down so too did several large banks which almost overnight dragged the State of Connecticut into a two-year recession. Some $300 million had evaporated. Although this financial earthquake was dwarfed by the Bernie Madoff scandal two decades later, at the time it was devastating to the Connecticut economy.

When the dust settled, two of the partners landed in federal prison with terms of 7 and 9 years. The former chief financial officer was charged with embezzling $6 million. But he never saw the inside of a prison cell. He committed suicide before his trial began. A half dozen others connected to this group also went to prison.

To say that I was unaware of the company's shenanigans would not be entirely true. Over my three-year stint with the company there were plenty of rumors about insurance fraud and exaggerated property values to secure larger and larger mortgages.

Perhaps I was not smart enough to understand the entire story. Or maybe I simply turned a blind eye to it all. My job was to lease empty space in their buildings. I had nothing to do with their financial relationships with banks or their investors. But I never asked hard questions either.

I could see the handwriting on the wall and I left just before the company crashed and burned. I mistakenly thought that the lenders (banks and insurance companies) would be anxious to hire me to help sort out their commercial properties.

I could not have been more wrong.

For the next 18 months I was unable to find work. I went through all my savings and cashed out my retirement account. I was painting houses to supplement my unemployment check, barely squeaking by. I had recently recovered from a heart attack. And had just gotten divorced. My money was gone. And I was now a single parent of two teenage boys. The future looked dim.

I then got a call from a friend who needed help leasing some small shopping centers.

So, with a borrowed typewriter, the computer at the local library and a $5,000 loan from my father, I started a leasing business from my kitchen table. Before long I moved my office to an upstairs bedroom.

I did what I knew best, work with smaller 'mom and pop' businesses. And my business grew rapidly. Over the next 30 years I completed more than 600 transactions. I was a sole proprietor handling the marketing, sales, clerical and bookkeeping duties. I even installed my own signs. Though most were slightly crooked. But I liked working alone, and having the freedom to work from my home.

Looking back on my work life it is clear to me that my career was mostly unplanned. There was a lot of luck involved. But I do realize that the harder I worked, the luckier I got.

I am now retired from the real estate business and trying my hand at writing. This is my second book. But I am not ready to call myself an author just yet. I'm just a guy sharing my stories.

17

— • —

POLICE CAMP

We were finally scheduled for our first vacation. My dad, who was a NYC policeman, had an entire week off in the summer, which was rare. It was time to get out of the city for our very first family vacation.

It was the late 1950's. My family was in the middle of the post war baby boom. I was 7. My brother Andy was 9. My little sister Amy was a toddler. Tom would come along a couple of years later completing the Litsky family unit.

We lived modestly on a cop's salary, which in those days was enough to put food on the table and a roof over our heads. We had an old B&W Philco TV in the basement that we barely watched. Most of the time we were outside. Bouncing a 'Pensy Pinkie' rubber ball against a stoop or a wall. We also played tag. Kick the can. And ring-a-levio, the rules of which changed each time we played.

Our neighborhood was full of small, brick Cape style homes, fourteen almost identical houses on each side of the street. The blocks were laid out in a grid pattern. There were countless numbers of kids playing outside. That was life in Cambria Heights, a working-class neighborhood in Queens.

Most of the dads worked for the City. Our neighbors were firemen, bus drivers, sanitation workers and such. My dad was one of two cops living on our street.

When we were told that we were going on vacation for a week that summer I had trouble understanding why anyone would want to leave the paradise I called 233rd street. Afterall we were just a couple of blocks from the schoolyard at PS 176, offering us acres of black asphalt to play on.

But my parents thought we needed fresh, country air. I didn't know what that meant. Could we be going to another country?

Off we went in my grandparent's 1951 Dodge my dad borrowed for the vacation. My grandfather didn't drive much anymore. They lived in the Bronx where they could find pretty much anything they wanted within walking distance.

Though the car was the same age as me it was still shiny. It looked brand new since it had hardly been driven.

We loaded the car with our suitcases. Three of us piled into the back seat with our traveling toys. Andy had crayons and books. I had little toy plastic soldiers. Amy had rattles and things that squeaked. She liked to make noise. She still does.

Of course, there were no seatbelts. No child restraints of any kind. This was the 1950s.

It was a hot July afternoon. My dad cracked the windows which allowed air to flow in once we hit the highway. That was our air conditioning. We were off to the 'country.'

We were headed to Police Camp. Yes. Police Camp. It sounded rather ominous.

The camp was operated by the Police Benevolent Association to give NYC cops and their families a chance to get out of the City - into the fresh air the Catskill Mountains offered. It was an inexpensive vacation. Thirty dollars per week for adults and half that for children, which included 3 meals per day served family style in the enormous banquet hall.

It was an hour and a half drive from our home in Queens. This was the furthest I'd ever been away from home. My little sister Amy threw up in the car before we hit the Bronx. And then again just as we got to our destination. Andy and I spent our time fighting over something unimportant, teasing each other as brothers two years apart usually do. My parents squabbled on the best way to get there.

Looking back, had I been my dad I would have driven into a bridge abutment. But he was a better man than I.

Finally, after what seemed like forever to this seven-year-old, we arrived. We drove past a giant statue of a uniformed Patrolman with a young boy that had graced the entrance of the property since the 1930s.

The model for the young boy was former NY Mayor Fiorello La-Guardia's son. That very statue is now on display at NYC Police Head-quarters called One Police Plaza. Or One PP.

One PP made me laugh as a child. It kind of still does.

We had two connecting rooms with a shared bath in the 3-story wooden hotel structure comprising several hundred rooms. During the week that followed, two things stood out and remain in clear detail all these decades later.

The swimming pool. And a pool table in the bar.

Shortly after we settled in, we changed into our bathing suits, grabbed our towels and walked down the hill to a large cement pool of water. It was a hot day. I had never seen a swimming pool before. On hot days we would occasionally drive to Jones Beach and splash in the ocean. But this was truly an odd site. A swimming pool. What a concept. What will they think of next?

The pool was completely full, mostly with children. I learned to swim that week. The pool was spring fed, so it was very, very cold. Except for some warm spots. At the time, I didn't know where the warm spots came from, or I never would have put my face in that water.

A few days later Andy and I along with a couple of friends we met wandered into the empty bar. There was a large green table with holes in the corners and balls with numbers on top. Someone said it was a pool table. I assumed it was some kind of game for the cops to play.

A cube of blue chalk caught our attention. It looked like a cool thing to have. But to have it, we would have to steal it. There we stood, four children of cops in a huge hotel full of cops. We conspired. Daring each other to take it. I'm not sure which of us pulled off the caper but once we got outside the blue cube of chalk ended up in my pocket. We agreed to take turns holding on to it. My day was first. I already felt a huge sense of guilt having never stolen anything before. That, combined with the fear that I'd be caught and sent to reform school, left me numb.

Two cops passed me walking down the hall and asked if I had fun shooting pool. I was stunned. They must be mind readers. Or cops have special abilities to detect criminals.

I sat outside on one of the Adirondack chairs on the porch and another cop asked me if I was good at shooting pool. Again, I was too stunned to respond. These cops were simply amazing. After this happened a third time, I was one sufficiently freaked out seven-year-old. I was scared --- and I had to pee.

After I flushed, I washed my hands and caught a glimpse of myself in the mirror. All became clear. Unbeknownst to me, one of the guys had chalked the tip of my nose which left a perfect blue dot on the end of my snout.

I washed it off and strolled back into the bar area. I returned the stolen chalk to the pool table and breathed a huge sigh of relief. Right then and there I promised myself I would never steal anything ever again.

I kept that word for about five years. Until a Milky Way bar from Adeline's candy store on Linden Blvd. found its way into my pocket.

At the end of the week, we headed home. Andy had left his crayons on the ledge behind the car's rear seats. Over the course of our weeklong vacation, the crayons had melted in the hot July sun trapping in its wake a platoon of my half melted plastic soldiers. My dad started the car and twenty minutes later Amy tossed up her lunch again. Maybe twice. But looking back, it was just awful.

On the ride home we ate Animal Crackers and other cookies. And sipped milk from containers with straws. Some of it spilled on the fabric seats along with cookie crumbs. And a bag of popcorn. My Hershey Bar melted in my hands which of course I wiped on the back of the seat in front of me. Andy's side of the car didn't look any better.

When we arrived back in the city my grandfather didn't want his car back. He said he was ready to give up driving anyway. Even at seven I knew that wasn't completely true.

We totally trashed my grandfather's car.

18

O CANADA

Quick. What are the lyrics to the first line of the Canadian National Anthem? I didn't know it either and I've been to many hockey games.

The first line of the beautiful anthem is, *"O Canada. Our home and native land."*

A generation after my first family vacation at Police Camp I found myself tight on cash with a wife and two kids ages 8 and 9 in need of a summer vacation. We made plans to drive to Nova Scotia in our Toyota minivan.

The silver minivan with its angled front end looked like the front car of the Disneyland monorail. It sat 7 in three rows. Since we had extra space, my mother-in-law and my wife's uncle Domenic asked if they could come along for the ride. They said they'd pick up the tab for the vacation, so it was a 'win-win.' A free vacation. What could go wrong?

My mother-in-law was a quiet woman who liked to go for rides. Neither she nor Domenic had ever been more than a few hours from the home they shared with their three other aging unmarried siblings in Providence. An entire book could be written about that. But that is not my story.

Domenic was a rolly-polly guy in his mid-60's. He had a slight stutter and a full head of pure white hair. He repeatedly told stories of his youth during the Great Depression. Stories I heard at each visit. For all intents and purposes, he was my father-in-law. And I enjoyed him enormously.

We packed up the ridiculously looking van. Most of our stuff was bungie-corded to the roof rack. Off we headed north to Bar Harbor, Maine to catch the overnight ferry to Yarmouth, Nova Scotia.

I drove and Domenic rode shotgun. My wife and mother-law took the second and third row of seating. Each with a child. We knew enough to keep our two rambunctious children separated.

They are just a year apart and had always found ways to tease and annoy the crap out of each other. And me.

On paper this was a good plan. A half hour into our five and a half-hour drive to Bar Harbor, Domenic started to read highway signs. Out loud.

Not only the names of each city we passed from Pawtucket to Portland. But billboards as well. Every billboard. Fast food restaurants. Gas and lodging. And every cigarette brand you could think of. Out loud. He was driving me crazy.

The children, though separated by a row of seating, found ways to hit each other or throw things. Their mother frequently let out an earth-shattering scream for them to stop.

Just as I was considering pulling over to hitch-hike home, I saw the sign for Bar Harbor.

We pulled our overstuffed vehicle onto the ferry and settled in for our overnight trip. Three miles out in international waters the casino opened. My youngest, Jonathan, borrowed a quarter from his grandmother.

Before we knew it, he put it into a slot machine ignoring the prominently displayed MUST BE 18 TO PLAY sign. A moment after he pulled the handle three cherries appeared. And then $40 in quarters loudly clanked into the metal tray below. Bells rang and lights twirled. A lot of attention was drawn to him. I quickly grabbed up the money so there would be no issue with his underage gambling.

The battle then ensued. He wanted his money. And his brother wanted to put his own quarter into the one-arm bandit.

I cannot remember how we resolved this, but we all settled in for the night in three tiny rooms. The mom and grandmother each took a child. And after driving all day, I was ready for a good night's sleep. I was sharing my tiny room with Domenic.

Just as I was nodding off Domenic started to snore. He kept me up all night listening to his sounds alternating from snoring to farting. Some of them sounded the same. My love for this man was beginning to wane.

We docked in the morning. Set to enjoy the next five days circumnavigating the beautiful island of Nova Scotia.

As we drove off the Ferry, Domenic spotted the "WELCOME TO CANADA" sign. And he let out in his best singing voice the first two words of the Canadian National Anthem which is also its name.

"O Canada" and nothing else rang out from his voice about every ten minutes. From the beautiful village of Peggy's Cove. To Halifax. Then up and around the rocky coast of Cape Breton Island where I wanted to jump into the cold North Atlantic and end this torture. And finally, back to Yarmouth for our return ferry ride to Maine.

"O Canada" every ten minutes. For five days. And five nights. Over hundreds of scenic miles.

His last *"O Canada"* was uttered upon reentering the U.S. I only had five hours more until I dropped them off in Providence. A couple of hours after that and I'd finally be home.

Then it started again.

'Portland, 10 miles.' 'Gas and Lodging just ahead.' 'McDonald's next exit.' 'Soft Shoulder.' 'Winston Tastes Good.'

You get the idea. And then finally, the only sound from him was his blissful snoring. Everyone else in the car was asleep, too.

We pulled into Providence and dropped them off near midnight. We were finally back at our home in Connecticut a little after 2 am. I dragged myself into bed with my teeth unbrushed and my clothes mostly on.

I had been asleep about four hours when the phone rang. It was my boss's secretary.

*"Hope I didn't wake you. But Michael needs you to be in Miami for meetings today. Your ticket is at the airport (*you could do that back then*). Can you make a 9:00 am flight?"*

"Sure," was all I could muster.

I grabbed a few clothes and my toiletries and was out the door in a half hour.

When my plane landed, I called our Miami office and had them reschedule the meetings until the following day. I placed a 'do not disturb' sign on my hotel room doorknob. Finally. No kids. No wife. No in-laws.

I fell sound asleep in my hotel room for the next nine hours. It was the highlight of my vacation.

19

CANCUN, MEXICO

I was on a chaise lounge poolside lost in my daydreams under a bright Caribbean sky. Off in the distance I could see the white triangular sails dotting the calm azure colored sea.

The warm sun and the gentle cool breeze were in perfect balance. There was just enough rum, shaved ice and pineapple juice in my Piña Colada to help take the edge off my memory of the two-year nightmare called the Covid-19 pandemic.

My large family came through it physically unscathed. It will be some years before we can calculate the emotional toll it took on all of us. With few exceptions, we hadn't seen each other for more than two years.

My youngest granddaughter had never met most of her family. Knowing them only by pictures displayed in our living room. And occasional visits via Zoom and FaceTime.

Having missed two years of holidays, graduations and birthdays, we were a family in need of a gathering

And so, we gathered.

None of us have a home large enough so we gathered at an all-inclusive resort in Cancun, Mexico.

Twenty-one of us (from ages two to 75) shared a week of tears, hugs and laughter.

My wife, siblings, our four children and four grandchildren. Nieces and nephews. My Mexican in-laws and nephews. One big mushy, huggy, loving family. Together. It was a slice of heaven.

Only my youngest brother Tom was unable to get away due to other commitments. We made him the "designated survivor."

As I sat on my chaise lounge, I thought about my grandparents who sailed from Europe with all their earthly belongings in suitcases not much larger than what we brought to Mexico for a week's vacation.

I wondered what they would have thought about this large and loving family three generations later. I thought about my first family vacation at Police Camp. And the time I drove my young family too many miles around Nova Scotia.

The key ingredient to a successful family vacation is to bring with you a heart full of love. With no expectations.

Just then I was splashed with a cup of water.

"Hey grandpa. Come play with me," my two-year-old granddaughter Juno commanded.

Into the water we went.

20

— · —

ON THE STREET WHERE I LIVE

There was a slight burning smell in my home, and I was concerned that it could be the beginning of an electrical fire. The scent was barely perceptible but present, nevertheless.

I dialed the fire department and asked that a firefighter come over. With hopes that he'd reassure me this was more my imagination than a potential conflagration. The operator said someone would be over shortly.

I live in a small suburban town in northern Connecticut. Fire issues here are handled by the Volunteer Fire Department. They respond to all fire and rescue emergencies. It was a quiet fall evening in a town where a quiet evening is the default setting. Not much happens here, particularly at night.

I waited on my front porch for a firefighter to come by to tell me I was overreacting.

Ten minutes later I heard a fire engine off in the distance. Then another. And another. I assumed that there must be a fire somewhere close by.

A few moments later my street was filled with half a dozen engines of all shapes and sizes. The sky lit up with the red flashing lights. And it was loud. Everyone in my neighborhood was up and out of their homes.

Some brought out their own lawn chairs to watch the excitement. A dozen or more firefighters rushed forward, grabbing hoses, axes and other equipment then paused to await orders to storm into the house. My house. It looked like an invading force.

But it lacked one critical element. Fire. Nothing was on fire.

After a few minutes everyone calmed down and I pulled the chief aside. He and I along with four senior fire officers came into my kitchen to smell the outlets to identify the cause.

We then marched through my home, room by room. Turning on the lights with each of us smelling the electrical outlets. I led fully outfitted firefighters through my house, each of us taking turns smelling the wall outlets. I later was told it was an amusing sight from the outside of my house, where neighbors sat on lawn chairs to enjoy the commotion.

It took a while until we determined that it was my dishwasher. To save energy I turned off the heating element which dries the dishes at the end of its cycle. I had inadvertently pushed the button to the ON position when I had run it earlier that evening.

This was the first time using the heating element on a 4-year-old dishwasher. When the heating element came on it burned off some dust that had settled since its installation. And it briefly smelled a little like an electrical fire.

Disappointed there was no fire to fight, the firefighters headed back to their trucks. They hung up their protective gear and put away the axes. Several minutes later the trucks retreated from my street and returned to their fire houses. Neighbors lingered a bit longer exchanging gossip. But they soon departed.

And just like that my street was quiet. The dark night air once again filled by the evening sounds from a quiet street in a small town. Nothing but crickets and chirps.

I grew up in Queens where your neighbor's house was just 10 feet away separated by a driveway just wide enough to squeeze a car through. As a kid I played in the street or at the asphalt playground behind our elementary school four blocks away. Neighborhood houses were on postage sized lots with a small lawn and a tree in the front. Pretty typical of post-war, single-family housing in the1950s.

The neighborhood I now live in encompasses streets with four-bedroom homes and two-car garages set on half-acre lots. Lawns are a big deal in suburbia. I was 27 when I moved here. I had no experience with lawns. But that was obvious. My house had the worst lawn on the street. And I had 'Lawn Envy.'

To fit in better with my new neighbors I bought a bag of the highest quality fertilizer I could find. I was told it was used by the finest golf courses in the land. That was good enough for me. I am to this day a trusting and gullible consumer.

I carefully spread the fertilizer up and down my large lawn. A week later after a good soaking rain, I had a lawn with bright green stripes. Undeterred, the next weekend I returned to the garden store and purchased yet another bag of this super expensive, super fertilizer. This time I carefully spread it from side to side.

Yup, you guessed it. I had a checkerboard lawn. This delighted the children on the street who made up games to play on my ridiculous front lawn. A bit later in the season the owner of a lawn maintenance company knocked on my door. He said my lawn was so horrible he offered the first two applications for free if he could use before and after photos in his advertising.

Problem solved.

21

GOOD NEIGHBORS

Not a conversation was had with my neighbor without him mentioning his gas mileage. He meticulously kept track of it, and loved to share this information with anyone who would listen.

I kept a five-gallon gas can in my garage for my lawn mower. One day I secretly began putting increasingly more gas in the tank of my neighbor's car. It was fun to see how excited he got each week as his gas mileage increased from 28 mpg to 35 mpg. At 40 mpg he was beside himself and went on and on about what a fantastic car he had.

When his car reached an incredible 60 mpg, he wrote to Volkswagen hoping to be featured in a television ad. I then realized I went too far and reduced the amount of extra gas I was putting in his tank. Within a few weeks his mileage was back to normal. I never said a word. And he finally stopped talking about his damn gas mileage.

I have a big back yard and thought it would be fun to put in a garden. Since every garden needs good soil, I ordered a load of cow manure.

Two days later a truck dropped a pile of cow shit on my driveway. It was the size of my Subaru. And it was disgusting. It stunk up the entire neighborhood. It took a full weekend to shovel it one wheelbarrow at a time to my back yard. The odor lingered for weeks.

Being from Queens I knew nothing about gardening. I had never grown anything. So I took the advice of others. Tomatoes and Zucchini. Easy to grow.

I put in ten tomato plants of different varieties. And then made ten small hills for zucchini plants. Four seeds in each hill. Yes. Your math is correct. That would be forty zucchini plants with each plant yielding 10-12 zucchinis. Or four to five hundred zucchinis. Who knew?

We were soon overwhelmed by zucchinis. We fried them. Baked them. Made salads and breads. Used them as noodles in lasagna. And on Kabobs. We gave away all that we could. But simply couldn't keep up. If I didn't pick them each day, they would continue to grow. Several became the size of baseball bats. My little 'victory garden' was becoming a nightmare.

Finally, I surrendered. My boys, then 7 and 8, and I picked all that remained and pulled the plants. We dragged their wagon full of zucchinis up the street. At each house we put a couple of zucchinis in the mailbox until the zucchinis were finally gone.

I still don't like zucchini. But every time I see one, I smile thinking about my kitchen once overflowing with them.

Tomatoes were a different story. Planted in soil rich with manure these plants took off. Within weeks the plants were enormous. I wasn't concerned with an abundance of tomatoes. Making a pasta sauce requires a lot of them.

My neighbor asked me to look after his garden while they were out of town. He did not possess a green thumb. His garden looked anemic with most of his plantings contemplating suicide.

In his absence I put several shovels of my cow-shit rich soil in his garden, and replaced his four nearly dead tomato plants with the best of mine. I thought I owed him something for screwing around with his gas mileage.

I happened to be in my driveway when he returned at the end of the week. He screeched with delight seeing his garden blooming.

"Look what I did! This is a hell of a garden. I knew I could do it!" he yelled to his wife who was unloading their car. She was always smarter than him. She looked at me, rolled her eyes and smiled. Mouthing the words, *"Thank you."*

In those years I worked in an advertising agency. We were doing a promotion of some sort for a client which required an appearance of a gorilla. My task was to rent a full-body gorilla suit.

A friend down the street had constructed a large backyard playscape for his children. It was eight feet off the ground, with climbing ropes. Ladders and swings. He referred to it as a Jungle Gym.

How could I resist. I donned the gorilla suit. And monkey-walked across several back yards to his house. I was followed by a slew of kids screaming with laughter. I climbed to the top of the playscape and pounded my chest like King Kong on the Empire State Building.

I could see his wife through the glass patio door talking on the phone. Her back was turned away from me. She hung up and turned clearly annoyed at the racket the kids were making in her yard. And then she saw me and nearly fainted.

I swung down the apparatus. Threw one of the small children over my shoulder. And ran out of her view. It was one funny moment. And then I realized someone might shoot me. Although we live on a quiet suburban street, several of my neighbors were hunters. Therefore, there were guns in their homes. And what hunter wouldn't like to bag a large ape in their backyard?

So, I took off the gorilla's head and returned the child to her yard. We all laughed about it for weeks.

There were a lot of children on my street in those days. Most of them within a narrow age span of three-to-four-years. They were loud and creative. They were all good kids who got into a normal amount of trouble.

That is until they stole the ice cream truck.

One summer afternoon the neighborhood children were playing outside. From a block away you could hear the obnoxious sounds of "Turkey in the Straw" booming through speakers announcing that the ice cream truck was headed this way. Children ran to the street with money in hand and waited with anticipation.

By the time the truck pulled up and stopped in front of my house a dozen children already formed a line. I took a moment to admire how well-mannered these youngsters were as they took turns buying their favorite summer treats. I went back to my household chores unaware of what was about to happen.

The older boys (ages 10-12) were last to be served. One ordered an ice cream sandwich but instead of paying he took off running. The ice cream man, more like an older teenager, flew out of the door of his truck and gave chase leaving the engine still running.

Several of the neighborhood kids hopped in and put the truck in drive. They headed up the street at a glacial speed with the obnoxious music still playing.

Meanwhile, the ice cream man gave up trying to catch the speedy young-ster and now gave chase to the kids in his truck. A few moments later the young felons realized that we live on a cul de sac....a dead-end street. No one thought that far ahead.

So, they applied the brakes. Put the truck in park. Jumped out. And ran into the woods never to be caught.

There was snow on the ground before any of the parents in the neigh-borhood heard that story. It went unreported to Simsbury's finest. No one was hurt. In a display of particularly poor parenting, I let it slide. Mostly because I couldn't think of a good punishment since the thought of this caper made me laugh. And it still does.

Winter turned to spring. And then spring to summer complete with all the usual sounds and smells. However, there was one thing missing. No "Turkey in the Straw" being played ad nauseam.

For the next six years no ice cream truck appeared on our street.

So, what became of our gang of young felons? Among them there is a film maker. A doctor. A teacher. A financial analyst. A stockbroker. And, of course, a policeman.

Some forty years later I still live in the house where I raised my boys. I share it with my second wife whose two children spent their best years here, as well. We now have grandchildren running about.

I refinanced this house five times over the years to pay for colleges and weddings. My current mortgage should be fully paid off about the time I turn 96.

And each summer I still enjoy a treat from the man who plays "Turkey in the Straw."

22

PUTTING THE **FU** IN FUNERAL

I don't like funerals. But as I get older, I am finding myself at more of them.

I lost a work friend a while back. I wouldn't say we were close. But we did share lunches together a few times a week for years. So, I put on my darkest suit and my most somber tie and attended his funeral.

I was surprised at how many people were crowded into the funeral home. They all seemed to know each other. I knew no one there except for my horizontal friend.

The eulogy was sweet. Most of us shed a tear as my friend's years on this planet were summed up with a mix of interesting moments and funny stories.

When the funeral concluded I walked solemnly to my car. I had no interest in going to the cemetery. I'm not much of a cemetery guy. I planned on heading back to my home/office to finish my workday.

My cell phone rang just as I started my car. It was a small work issue that could wait. I am easily distracted and don't multitask very well. I have a bit of ADD. Admittedly, it is an annoying but a sometimes-charming characteristic.

It was lightly misting so I put on my headlights and wipers as I concluded the phone call. I made a right turn out of the driveway. Five blocks later I noticed a line of cars behind me. I didn't know the cemetery was in this direction.

I soon realized that they were following me. While being distracted with my phone call, I must have cut in front of someone exiting the funeral home's parking lot. And I ended up leading a small parade of mourners.

I pulled over into a supermarket parking lot followed by a line of seven or eight cars. I hopped out and told the driver of the car immediately behind me that I was not headed to the cemetery. I was going home.

Clearly frustrated he blasted me with a couple of F-bombs as though this was somehow my fault. Riding shotgun in his Camry was a white-haired old lady. She held my gaze for a moment as I shrugged my shoulders proclaiming my innocence.

She wore a tense and angry face and slowly raised up her fist and flipped me the bird, as she mouthed what I could do to myself.

Thus, confirming that you cannot spell funeral without FU.

23

—·—

IT IS THE JOURNEY - NOT THE DESTINATION

The plane banked left. From my window seat I could see the wide arc of the Hawaiian Islands dotting the blue Pacific below. This breathtaking sight caused me to say to my seatmate,

"Wow, looks just like the map in my Atlas."

He looked at me like I was an idiot and went back to his book.

This was my first trip to Hawaii. Ten days in paradise on the island of Maui. I was visiting a friend who had moved there a year earlier.

She found me a room to rent nearby. While she was at work I explored the beautiful island in my rented Jeep. We made plans to hang out several evenings and take a weekend trip to the far side of the island with a friend of hers.

It was January and I was in paradise. Back home it was snowing. Poor cold bastards. I was under a palm tree enjoying watching surfers tackle four-foot waves. It sucks to be everyone else.

This is the season when some 10,000 humpback whales (the world's densest population) migrate from Alaska to the warm shallow waters of Maui. My tour book said that it is common for these 25 to 40-ton creatures to breach from the water creating a thunderous splash. They are a spectacular sight to behold.

This I had to see in person.

I sat myself on the port side of the tour boat since it was the sunny side. We were told that whale watching can be hit or miss. Sometimes you don't get to see anything. If I don't see a whale at least I'd catch a nice tan.

A woman sat down next to me dragging a large hard case. As we pulled from the dock, she proceeded to set up her photographic rig. She had three cameras. One with a large lens on the tripod. Two smaller ones hung from her neck. This was a woman on a mission.

I sat quietly with my thoughts. With my hand held camera at the ready. Enjoying the warm afternoon.

An hour later without warning a whale breached not more than 50 feet from our boat. It went straight up and hung in the air in what seemed like forever. A little like one of Michael Jordan's spectacular airborne slam-dunks. It seemed impossible to hang in the air for that long. I stood with my mouth open amazed at the power and beauty of this gigantic creature.

I was so in awe of this moment I forgot to take a picture. Yet it remains imbedded in my memory bank forever.

The woman next to me spent the rest of our tour sullen and pissed off. She missed the shot.

"What a waste of time and money," she bitched.

At the end of the day, I had a sweet memory and a nice tan. I watched her angrily load her oversized camera case into her rental car. I picked up a post card from the gift shop of a whale breaching. Pretty much like the one I had just seen.

The days that followed were filled with exploration. Driving around the island. Snorkeling off sun-soaked beaches. Hiking around the volcanic crater atop Mount Haleakala. And strolling around the picturesque town of Lahaina. Where I parked in a two-decker garage made famous by Joni Mitchell's song lyric ,*"They paved paradise and put up a parking lot."*

That weekend my friend Carla, her friend Judith and I headed off to Hana on the eastern shore of Maui. We drove the legendary Road to Hana. This 52-mile road winds through incredible rainforests. Flowing waterfalls. And dramatic seascapes. This is not a road to take if you are in a hurry. There are more than 600 curves and dozens of bridges. Some spots are only wide enough for a single vehicle.

You want to take this ride slowly. Not so much because it can be dangerous at a higher speed. But this spectacular road needs to be enjoyed at a slower pace.

Judith is a native of the island. She knew the road well. An hour into our drive she asked me to pull over to a spot just large enough to park our Jeep.

She motioned us to follow her on a slightly worn footpath. A quarter of a mile in from the road was an amazing view. Like a photo you'd see on a nature calendar. A waterfall dropped its contents fifty feet below into a pool of water about the size of a basketball court.

We stood in awe. Our senses bombarded by the scent of tropical flowers, the warmth of sunshine and the welcoming sound of water falling.

"Let's go skinny dipping," Judith said as her clothes came off.

Just to be clear, these were platonic friends. Nothing romantic was going on. That made the moment even odder. Remembering that since my divorce I promised myself new experiences, I dropped my pants and jumped in naked as the day I was born.

We were frolicking in the middle of nowhere being showered by a giant waterfall. And then we heard voices.

"This shit only happens in the movies," I said under my breath.

We could see a young couple with three kids heading our way. They were approaching toward the direction of our pile of clothing. We waded into chest high water. And waited to see what would happen. A quick glance was all they needed. They came within about 10 yards when they stopped. Our pile of clothing revealed a couple of bras and my underwear.

The water was also clear and didn't hide anything.

If I read their body language correctly, he wanted to stay, and the children wanted to swim. But she pointed them in another direction and away they went in a huff.

And we laughed.

An hour later we arrived in Hana for the evening. The house was beautiful but isolated. Built in the middle of the jungle.

There isn't much to do in Hana. It is quiet and secluded. Perhaps that's what brought former Beatle George Harrison here. In the years since his death other celebrities have built large homes, much to the consternation of the locals.

For me, The Road to Hana is a perfect metaphor for life. It is a beautiful reminder that it is not the destination that is important.

It is the journey.

24

My Own Personal Woodstock

I don't know if it was Crosby, Stills, Nash or Young who told their audience at Woodstock that they were, *"scared shitless"*, but some decades later I knew the feeling. Of course they were playing before an audience of half million. Mine was a bit smaller.

With my acoustic guitar in hand, I paused for a moment before walking up the steps to the stage. Out in the open field were 300 or so waiting for my 15-minute set of original songs.

I could hardly believe I was actually going to share a few songs I'd written with people I didn't know. How the hell did I get here?

I taught myself how to play the guitar when I was in Junior High School. In those days songs were pretty simple. Three chords. Three verses. And a chorus.

I purchased songbooks of my favorite artists trying hard to mimic their voices and guitar work. I did it badly. But then, I was an audience of one.

Sometime in college, I began jotting down my own songs. I used my guitar to process whatever happened to be on my mind. My writing would start with a stream of consciousness while strumming some chord progressions. It was cheap therapy in the privacy and solitude of my living room.

A score of years later I had written some 50 songs. Most were crap. But a few I believed were pretty good. And I wanted to hone my songwriting skills.

I joined the Connecticut Songwriter's Association. The group is comprised of a mix of amateur and professional musicians. We shared our songs (on tape) and got honest feedback at the monthly meetings.

Over time my work improved. I was clever with my rhyming couplets. And as an advertising guy who wrote radio commercials, I knew how to find and use a good hook.

We were invited to play a free concert at Hubbard Park in Meriden, CT. Each musician would have 15 minutes of original music – about three songs.

I was the fourth to step on stage that day. The three players I had to follow were really good. I took careful note of how close each one stood to their mikes. One for vocal and one for guitar. And I admired the ease of how they introduced themselves and related to the audience.

They were wonderful. And now it was my turn.

My hands were shaking, and my mouth was dry. I remember hearing once that you can bite down gently on your tongue to salivate. In my nervousness I bit down too hard. Now my eyes were watering, too.

To quote Elvis, *"It's now or never"* and my shaky legs took me up four steps. There was nothing else on stage but me and a couple of skinny microphones to stand behind. There was simply no place to hide. And 300 people were watching my every move.

I didn't know how to do this so I was honest. And I made them my friends.

"Hi, I'm Eric Litsky. And I've never played outside of my living room. I've been writing songs for 20 years and I'd like to share a couple of them with you today."

I had their attention. And helped to set their expectations low. Of course, I didn't tell them I also had to pee.

I played a sweet song about my grandfather coming to America – along with two funny songs. One about divorce. The other about the Japanese buying America. Both timely topics of the day.

When I finished they clapped. I even got a whistle or two and a loud, *"Yeah, man!"* But those may have both come from my fellow songwriters. Songwriters are a supportive bunch.

I realized several things that day. People at a free concert on a beautiful afternoon are a forgiving audience. An audience will root for you if you are honest with them. They had never heard my music before. So they had nothing to compare it to. Though I am certain they would not have enjoyed me trying to cover a James Taylor song.

Once off stage the adrenaline rush gradually subsided. I was proud of myself that day. I had pushed myself way beyond my comfort zone and shared a part of me with complete strangers.

25

— • —

ART IS IN THE EYE OF THE BEHOLDER

S o long as you be holding your own painting.

My first visit to MOMA (The Museum of Modern Art) was to see a retrospective on Henri Matisse. I loved how the vibrant colors brought the subject matter to life in a playful, joyful way. I was hooked.

The very next day I purchased canvasses. Paints. Brushes An easel. And, of course, a French beret. I wanted to experience what it would be like to be a painter.

I knew I had little to no artistic talent. But this wasn't about creating a beautiful piece of art. It was about experiencing the artistic process. Without judgement.

So, I set up the easel and canvas and began to paint. Thoroughly enjoying putting colors on a canvas.

Honestly, I have always had trouble matching colors.

Without some guidance my clothes often don't match. And I am not allowed to wear the reddish/pinkish checkered sport jacket I love so much -- except in Las Vegas -- the only place on earth where I get compliments on my taste in loud clothes.

Originally priced at $495 at Jos. A. Bank (who I refer to as José Bank), I picked the sport jacket up for $25 at their annual *Let's Get Rid of Crap Nobody Wants Sale*.

But with a blank canvas in front of me I was free to create. I painted a dozen mostly geometric canvasses with bright primary colors. Several of them still hang in my garage above the rakes and shovels.

I would hazard to guess that Renoir's or Picasso's garages were not as interesting as mine.

And then I discovered what I really liked. Dripping and splashing paint like Jackson Pollock. Oh, what fun.

I placed canvases on my then unfinished basement floor and dripped and splashed. I made a glorious mess. Paint on me. Paint all over the floor. And some on the canvas. Eventually I found a technique that worked. And created what I think is a pretty good piece. Not to worry, Mr. Pollock. No competition here.

In my living room where we have several tasteful lithographs hanging. There is a truly priceless piece of art. An original Litsky.

Well, that is not entirely true. Though it is priceless to me. It did cost about 20 bucks in supplies and a $100 frame.

And of course, carpeting for my basement floor to cover splattered red paint that looked like a crime scene.

A few years ago, my sister Amy organized an outing for a bunch of us to a wine painting party. An instructor gave us step by step lessons on painting a lovely scene of woodlands on a fall day. Bright colors. Leaves falling. You get the picture.

With a glass of wine in one hand and a brush in the other we dutifully followed her directions. Our paintings of the fall foliage were dreadful. But we laughed joyfully. It was a great night.

My eight-year-old granddaughter Zoe recently came across my ugly painting while looking for something in our hall closet.

"Grandpa, why did you paint a picture of a forest on fire?"

Yes, it is a pretty good painting of a forest fire. But clearly not the tranquil fall foliage scene I was going for. Leaving me to wonder if renaming the subject can turn crap into a fine piece of art.

A lovely fall foliage or a blazing forest fire?

26

---•---

IT TAKES TWO TO TANGO

Why did the Jewish guy dance a Tango? It sounds like the beginning of a really bad joke.

I love the Tango. It pulls at your heart strings much like Klezmer, the traditional European Jewish music of my ancestors. It is raw emotion that commands movement. And like Klezmer, it is hard to listen to without wanting to get up and move.

The melancholy sound of the bandoneon – akin to the accordion - fills the air with music generating feelings that range from deep sadness to ecstatic joy. This is the same way I experience a first-class musician wailing the sounds of Klezmer on a clarinet.

Jews first arrived in Argentina after being expelled from Spain during the Inquisition. Mass Jewish immigration, along with the Italians started in the 1890's about the time the Tango was born in Buenos Aires' poor urban section of La Boca -- not to be confused with Boca Raton, which is on the Lower East Side of Florida, a bit north of Miami.

Tango is the music of the immigrant. And of the ghetto.

I grew up hearing Klezmer music. In my adult years I started listening to Tango. Both tell their stories with either Yiddish or Spanish lyrics. While I understand neither, I am nonetheless drawn to their unique sounds.

The Tango is passionate and sensual with rich expressions, improvisations, and close connection between dancers. Two bodies moving as one with grace. Slowly and playful at first, then quickening to a torrid pace. Simply put, it is lovemaking with your clothes on.

So, Tango was the music I chose to listen to as I cleaned my house and fixed dinner before my first date with Norma at my home. I vacuumed and dusted to the heavy downbeat of the rapid Milongas and complex rhythms of Astor Piazzola. And chopped and prepped the meal to the sweet vocals of Carlos Gardel. After a quick shower I opened a bottle of Spanish wine and waited with anticipation for the doorbell to ring.

I had met Norma a few weeks earlier through our mutual friend, Wendy. We had been out on just one date. A nice dinner and some music at a blues bar afterwards. I had been divorced for some time and looked forward to getting to know Norma better.

When we first met, I detected a slight accent. Because of her green eyes and light complexion, I guessed Czechoslovakia, but I was wrong by an ocean and a half. She is Mexican. Born and raised in Mexico City, she came to the States in her early 20s.

The doorbell rang. Norma was right on time and appeared a little overwhelmed. Not by the house, I'd spent most of the day cleaning. Or the meal I prepared. Or the flowers in the vase on my kitchen table. Or even the fire in the fireplace. No, it was the Tango CD. It took her breath away.

She had grown up listening to Tango. Her father called them 'Argentinian Operas.' Much like American country and western music, Tango lyrics tell simple and often sad stories of lost loves and of broken dreams. Encapsulated in a distinctive orchestration of sound and rhythm.

It was a successful date and our relationship flourished. Many months later I surprised her with a series of Tango lessons. And we danced.

A few years of lessons followed. Although we improved, neither one of us ever considered ourselves much more than a beginner. But we loved the music. Loved to dance. And our love blossomed.

We were inspired to visit Buenos Aires, home of the Tango. Despite its long history of political, social and economic turmoil, Buenos Aires is a vibrant and beautiful city, alive with the sounds of Tango. More than a dance, it is ingrained in the culture. It is the soul of the Argentinian experience.

There is Tango music everywhere.

We rented an apartment in the affluent section of Recoleta, a short walk to its famous cemetery where generations of elite porteños (those from Buenos Aires) lie in repose in their ostentatious mausoleums. Eva Duarte, (later Peron) who was beloved in Argentina and known throughout the world simply as 'Evita,' chose Recoleta as her final resting place.

Norma and I hit all the usual tourist spots. We marched with the Madres de los Desaparecidos (mothers of the disappeared) at Plaza de Mayo. Every Thursday afternoon the mothers march and mourn the thousands taken during the dictatorship in the 1970's. The Plaza is just across from Casa Rosada, the Pink House, (the seat of government) and the balcony where Evita waved to her adoring supporters.

We attended a Tango show at the famous Café Tortoni, where I was coaxed to briefly dance on stage with the star of the show. She made me look like a better Tango dancer than I actually am.

No trip to Buenos Aires is complete without attending a Milonga (Tango Dance). Milongas take place every night in all parts of the city. But this ain't no disco. These are for serious Tango dancers. They generally start late in the evening and end near sunrise. We arrived at 11:30 pm at a neighborhood Milonga in the Palermo section of the city, a short cab ride from our apartment.

We paid our modest admission fee and walked up a flight of stairs to a space the size of a high school gymnasium. The dance floor took up most of the huge room. It was surrounded by dozens of small tables and lots of chairs. We sat at a table off to the side. We were there more to watch than participate. After all we were and still are very much beginners.

There are unspoken rules about how to ask someone to dance. Brief eye contact. The slight nod of a head. An almost imperceptible motion of the hand. Each has meaning. And you must be careful because like an auction at Sotheby's, an inadvertent hand motion could end up becoming embarrassing.

We sat at our table making sure not to make eye contact with anyone since we did not know the rules of the Milonga. I have a habit of talking with my hands. On this night I sat on them.

After an hour we summoned up the courage to enter the dance floor. Entering a dance floor at a Milonga is like merging unto a highway. You look for an opening and dance your way in. All the movement is counter-clockwise.

We had picked up a couple of fancy moves in our dance classes. Back-wards movements. Close embraces. Leg kicks. And a few elaborate turns. These all work well with plenty of room around you. But not so much in a crowded, smokey milonga in the middle of the night.

Three minutes in I stepped on two women's feet. Norma did a spec-tacular kick nailing a male dancer next to us in the shin. Had we been cars on a highway there would have been a pile up. We toned down our movements and noticed that we were given a little extra space on the crowded dance floor. The other dancers handled us like drunk drivers at rush hour. L-O-T-S of room.

It is said that great tango dancers can complete movements in a space the not much larger than a chess board. I am generally pretty agile. But in that environment on that night, I felt awkward, clumsy and oafish.

We made it around the dance floor a couple of times and exited to our seats much to the relief of the other dancers. We sipped wine and enjoyed the music. When we left, about 1:30 am, there was a line of people still coming in.

Just another Tuesday night at a neighborhood Milonga in Buenos Aires.

I observed that porteños smoke too much. They are out into the wee hours of the morning dancing. They eat huge portions of meat and rarely a green vegetable. And they work all day in a cosmopolitan city with all the stress that it entails. Why aren't these good people all dead?

I think it has something to do with the power of the Tango. It is as if the music has a curative effect on one's health. And if the music is everywhere, there is wellbeing.

Tango on.

Tango dancing on a sidewalk in Buenos Aires.

27

Tap That

I hadn't been on stage since I was a child. Frankly, the very idea was terrifying. But as I entered my post-divorced life, I promised myself it would be filled with new experiences.

I joined a community theater group in my town so I could meet some new people. I probably shouldn't have been surprised when they actually asked me to get on stage.

The production was *Crazy for You* by George and Ira Gershwin. It's a silly song and dance show with music from the 1930s. Hopelessly out of date, it is charming with songs like "Embraceable You" and "I've Got Rhythm."

The show is known for its big tap-dancing numbers. As with most community theater groups this one was short on men. And this show called for men who could tap dance.

They asked me to join the dance line though I had no idea how to tap dance.

The first task was to buy size 10 ½ men's tap-dancing shoes. Not as easy as it sounds. These were the days before you could get practically anything on Amazon. I found myself wandering into a dance supply store, the kind that sells little girls' leotards and ballet tutus.

It felt creepy walking in. I'm not a guy who is comfortable shopping in stores that sell frilly and lacy little girls' accessories. Maybe it was just my imagination, but I believe the saleswoman and two other customers in the store were looking at me like I was a sex offender on the prowl.

Yuck!!!!

"How can I help you?" the sales lady said looking at me from over her bedazzled, red framed glasses.

"I'd like to buy tap dancing shoes."

"Would that be boys or girls?"

"Boys in black."

"And what size does your little boy wear?"

"That would be 10 ½ men's. And they are for me."

She gave me a quizzical look and pulled out a step ladder to reach a box at the tippy top of the shelf. Black Capezio's. Mens. Size 10 ½. She blew off the dust on the top of the box.

Out the door I went with my Capezio's tucked under my arm looking more like the Heisman Trophy than a middle-aged man on a mission to learn how to tap dance.

In three months' time I would be on stage in front of a paid, but forgiving audience, tap dancing to Gershwin's *"I Got Rhythm."* The problem was - - I got no rhythm.

Tap dancing is all about being light on your feet, as though a string is attached to the top of your head pulling you up toward the heavens. Just high enough to click your toes and heels on the floor, tapping and moving as directed.

It took a while for me to figure out my problem. I was moving a little like Frankenstein's monster. Amusing to watch perhaps, but not what the Gershwins or Miss Sheila, the choreographer, had in mind.

At that time, I also practiced Tai Chi, the ancient discipline of meditative movements. The imagery of these movements grounds you – toward the center of the earth.

Simply put, these two disciplines pulled me in opposite directions.

Once I put my Tai Chi practice on hold, my scuffle-ball-change improved. In no time at all I could *Shuffle off to Buffalo* without falling down or bumping the guy next to me.

When rehearsals finally began, I discovered two things. Neither of which should have been surprising.

First, no matter how hard I worked learning how to tap dance – I still sucked. They placed me in the second row hidden behind a really fat guy who was incredibly light on his feet.

Second, of the twelve tap dancing men on stage only two of us were straight. I had known gay people my entire life. I have always accepted them for who they are and never gave it a second thought.

But this was the first time that I was in the sexual minority. Indeed, I was the one out of step....no pun intended. It gave me pause. And a fresh appreciation of this very small slice of the gay community.

It served to make me a better man.

Miss Sheila directed us to look straight ahead and wear a self-assured smile.

"If you don't look at your feet no one else will either. You've got to sell it with a confident look," was her guidance.

When you think about it, that's pretty good life advice.

Our performance came and went. The audience loved our big tap number and gave us a huge ovation. I was well hidden behind a guy twice my size. And I didn't fall even once.

My tap shoes went into the back of my closet along with my bicycle shoes, hiking boots, cowboy boots and tango shoes. None of which I've worn in years.

Perhaps one day I will get to tap dance with one of my granddaughters.

28

WITTY WITNESS

The entire court room burst out laughing. It even put a smile on the face of an otherwise stoic judge.

It always pisses me off when a big guy bullies a small guy.

So, when I was asked to be an expert witness in a court case involving a landlord trying to stiff a fellow real estate broker out of his commission, of course, I enthusiastically said, *"Yes."*

This issue involved a fair amount of money. That is why we all ended up in a courtroom. A friend of mine who had a small real estate agency asked me to testify to support his claim. His attorney was a sole practitioner with a small practice. He was bright but inexperienced.

They were seriously overmatched by the landlord's attorneys. These guys were from a large downtown law firm. If you spoke the name of their firm quickly it sounded like a chair tumbling down a flight of stairs.

I had no experience in a real courtroom that looked eerily like the set of an episode of *Law and Order.* There was an attorney for the next case sitting behind me. He looked a bit like Sam Waterston. All very sobering.

The scowl on the judge's heavily lined face was intimidating. She looked like she hadn't moved her bowels in a month.

After an hour and a half of listening to the two attorneys argue I was bored, and my ass hurt. The wooden benches were not form fitting -- at least not to my form.

Finally, my guy's attorney called me. I was sworn in which was kind of cool.

He asked me a bunch of questions about my background and my opinion on the issue at hand. No need to get into the details of the case. It'll put you to sleep.

Then the landlord's attorney got up. He buttoned his tailored suit jacket and approached. An unnecessary theatrical gesture. That cinched it. I did not like this guy.

I anticipated that he would do his best to make an ass out of me. So, I was on guard for an adversarial assault.

He asked a lot of questions about what classes I had taken to become licensed. About continuing education. And about my overall knowledge of the laws regarding real estate and payment of commissions, etc. I won't bore you with those details either.

Then he got to the question to set me up for the knockout punch.

"Mr. Litsky, you've been a licensed real estate broker for over 30 years. You've completed numerous classes and seminars as required by the State of Connecticut. Therefore, you must know everything there is about real estate licensing."

"Well sir, I also have a driver's license. But I have no idea how far to park from a fire hydrant."

The courtroom burst out in laughter. The judge smiled as she smacked her gavel calling for order.

He yelled that I was unresponsive and wanted the answer stricken. Then he asked for a sidebar and the two attorneys approached the bench.

A moment later the judge said this was a good time for an afternoon break. Let's be back at 2:00 pm to resume.

"All Rise."

I was told I was done, and I could leave. Over the next hour they ended up making some kind of compromise. And that was the end of it.

I sent in a bill for my 3 hours' time. And no one ever called me again.

Law and Order is better.

29

FRYING PORK CHOPS NAKED

What struck me most about him was his breath. It was a blend of sardines and gin with a hint of cigar. His thinning, grey hair needed a brush as it flopped over his Lyndon Johnson-sized ears. The hair was so thick in those ears I was surprised he could hear anything at all.

He was an old man. Many years older than I am now. He sat next to me on the bench as I waited for the 7:15 train from New Haven to Windsor, Connecticut. It had been a long day for me. I had been in the City all day having just made the 4:15 Metro North from Grand Central by a whisker.

I now had an hour wait for my connecting train to take me to Windsor where I parked my car fourteen hours earlier. I was too tired to read yet too awake to snooze.

"Long day," was all he said hoping to lure me into a conversation to pass the time.

"Yeah. I caught the six am to the City this morning and I'm beat to hell."

"Boy, that brings me back. I was in and out of the City three times a week for almost forty years. Schlepping my sample case through the garment district. It was hell. But some days I really miss the action."

None of what he said about selling notions and fabrics was interesting to me. But he was a lonely guy and I had an hour to kill.

"*The wife and I had a nice place on the shore with a view of the Sound. I made a good living and raised my kids there. Cancer got her eight years ago. I now live in a retirement community of old farts over 55....more like over 75. But who's counting.*"

He sneezed twice in his handkerchief and I inched further away from him on the bench.

"*Were you in the City today?*" I asked.

"*Yeah. I go in once a week to see my daughter and grandson. He's now in high school and she's a nurse. Her prick of a husband took off last year with his bimbo secretary. He bought her a new pair of tits. The three of them took off with him to Florida.*

Florida. Let me give you some advice. Don't ever move to Florida. It's God's fucking waiting room."

I could sense he had a lot more to say about his family, work and life in general. But I think we were both relieved when the loudspeaker called his train.

"*I gotta go now. But you seem like a nice young man. So, I'll give you another piece of advice. Listen carefully.*"

He moved closer to me on the bench as if he was sharing a secret and hoarsely whispered, "*If you are dumb enough to fry pork chops naked, wear a fucking apron.*"

At first I found this line quite silly. But it stuck with me for all these years. And then I finally got it. It is a profound piece of advice from a strange old man I met for a few moments while waiting for a train.

30

— . —

THE BIGGEST BOOB ON A TOPLESS BEACH

We've now been friends for about 100 pages, so let me confess to a blind spot I have. One I am not proud of - but I am working on it.

I'm a Jewish guy born less than a decade after the Holocaust. I grew up in a multiethnic community in Queens. I enjoy diversity in my life and have had a lifetime of learning and appreciating cultures different from my own. I pride myself on being open and interested in people from all parts of the planet.

So, I was embarrassed at my behavior on a topless beach. But not for the reasons you might think. Here's the story.

The year I got divorced I took myself on my first solo vacation. Club Med - then known as the best place on the planet for singles.

I chose their Caravelle Resort on the tropical island of Guadeloupe in the French Caribbean. I didn't give it too much thought at the time. I just needed a place to destress. Club Med advertised itself as, *"an antidote for civilization."*

I had been through far too much civilization over that year. I was burnt out and desperately in need of a vacation.

What I hadn't realized at the time was that Guadeloupe is a French island. Hence topless sunbathing.

As I stretched out on my chaise lounge under a palm tree, my senses were assaulted in the most positive way. Caribbean blue water gently lapping up on the white sandy beach. And all around me topless women clad solely in itsy bitsy bikini bottoms.

I thought I died and went to Heaven.

I then spotted two amazingly beautiful women sunning themselves about 50 feet from me. They were long, lean, blonde, and of course topless. It took me a while to screw up my courage to walk over and say, *"Hello."* Recently divorced, I was a bit rusty at the dating scene. I hadn't been on a date since the Nixon administration.

But no one knew me here. So, if I made an ass of myself, so what. They were in animated conversation. I figured they were approachable since this was Club Med.

Over I went.

I got within about 10 feet and froze dead in my tracks. Their animated conversation was in German.

Maybe I had seen too many WWII movies or overheard too much about the Holocaust growing up. Clearly these two gorgeous twenty somethings had nothing to do with 1930's Germany. But in that moment, it didn't matter. I turned around and went back to my chaise lounge. Shame on me for being so closed minded.

And in that moment I was the biggest boob on the topless beach.

31

— · —

THE NOT SO WILD ONE

Geno's garage looked like a motorcycle showroom. There were new shiny bikes. And beat up antiques. Many colors, sizes and vintages. But everything was rideable. This is a man who loves to ride.

We live in Northern Connecticut where there is only about six months of good riding. If you are a motorcycle guy you want to get out on the road as soon as the weather breaks.

Geno loved everything about these bikes. What he didn't have was a regular riding partner. He knew that I rode a bicycle and that was powered by nothing but my legs. On a downhill, my speed would top out at around 20 mph.

"How would you like to go 60 or 70?" he would ask.

"Miles per hour!" I replied. *"I don't think so."*

One evening he made me a deal I couldn't refuse. The State of Connecticut offered a free program to teach its citizenry how to safely ride and care for motorcycles. In just one weekend you would learn enough to apply for a state permit, the first step in getting licensed.

Geno wanted to teach motorcycle safety and riding for them. In order for him to register to become a riding instructor he had to bring a student with him.

And that student was me.

The class was Friday night and all-day Saturday. In addition to training a dozen of us to ride, the classes also served to train their instructors. Each instructor presented a half hour section of the two-day course.

On Friday night we sat through lectures on safety and the rules of the road. We then straddled our chairs and imagined we were on real motorcycles. They showed us how to start, brake and engage gears on the invisible bike.

I made vroom-vroom sounds as I popped the clutch and put my chair into gear. In all modesty I was the best in the class that first night. I couldn't wait for the morning session to get on a real bike. This was going to be so much fun.

On Saturday morning we gathered in the large and empty community college parking lot. Where we found a dozen motorcycles and helmets lined up for us.

I got on the shiny black one.

We started them up. This was even more fun than riding the chair the night before.

The instructor had us ride in a straight line – about 50 yards – stop and turn around. We did this a few times. Wow! I was Marlon Brando in *The Wild Ones.* That is until I realized that the 175 cc motorcycle I was on was not much larger than the 10-speed Trek hanging up in my garage. But this sucker had a motor. My helmet could hardly contain my enormous smile.

The next instructor had us follow each other around in a large circle. First clockwise and then counterclockwise.

And then it was Geno's turn to instruct the class. I was so proud of my friend. And happy that I could be his guinea pig to help him become an official instructor.

His task was to have us do a ride in a figure eight pattern.

Perhaps you've had the experience of being a child on a school bus trip. Everyone is just fine until someone upchucks his breakfast. Showing his classmates that it is OK to throw up. And they do.

Such was the case with my figure eight. Halfway around the first turn, down I went. Geno frantically waved his hands for everyone to stop. But not before two others took my lead. And became one with the asphalt.

He got us settled down and we tried it again. And once again I went down. And let me tell you, at 10 mph asphalt hurts like hell. At 60 mph you are pretty much roadkill. That was it for me. I pushed my bike to the edge of the parking field and walked away while I still could.

Geno's half hour lesson was a disaster. He was not offered a position as an instructor and was pissed at me for weeks. But I'm pleased to say that our long friendship has endured.

I may not have gotten my motorcycle license, but I had my pride. When asked the next day why I was limping. I simply said that I crashed my motorcycle.

32

GRAND THEFT AUTO

I put on my blinker and made a right-hand turn. Just as I have done a thousand times in a thousand other places. A moment later there was a sheriff behind me with his lights flashing.

I was pretty sure you could make a turn on red. I remember getting ticketed years ago making a right on red in Connecticut. This was a few weeks before it was legal to do so.

I told the cop I was just practicing. Instead of letting me off with a smile and a warning, it cost me an extra $50 for being a smart ass.

I couldn't imagine the traffic laws being different here in Central Florida? In any case I decided to be on my best behavior.

I pulled over. A few moments later there were Sheriffs on both sides of our rented Nissan with hands on their guns. I little aggressive I thought for a minor traffic violation. I was as friendly as I could be.

"Good morning officer. What seems to be the problem."

"I'm Sheriff so and so. For your information video and audio of our conversation is now being recorded. I'll need to see your driver's license. It seems you are driving a stolen vehicle."

I looked at the camera in the center of his chest. I smiled and gave the friendliest little wave I could muster just in case this was played someday before an unfriendly audience.

"Officer. We picked up this car from Avis/Budget at Fort Lauderdale Airport 10 days ago. And we have been driving all over Florida this week," I said attempting to establish my un-felon-like behavior.

While it is a police officer's job to be in control of the scene – asking the questions, barking orders, etc., I was determined to control the mood of the moment. Keeping it light and respectful to ensure there would be no opportunity for any miscommunication.

The officer at my car window had his side arm, a second gun holstered across his chest and eight clips attached to his bullet-proof vest. He was armed to the teeth. I was armed with a toothy smile.

I had no fear of the Sheriffs. My dad was a cop. After I charmingly told him that my dad was *on the job*, I realized my dad would be over 100 today if he were still alive. No help there.

Two more Sheriff's cars soon pulled up to join in on what may have been the crime of the century here in this little town. I thought about Arlo Guthrie's "Alice's Restaurant." And then I heard the bark of a large dog coming from one of the cars. The officer wore a 'K-9' patch.

The thought of a police dog, however, did scare the crap out of me. I don't like German Shepherds. I watched far too many WWII movies.

Also, earlier that week we brought some 'THC-laden edibles' (legal in Connecticut) to an 80-year-old friend we visited. Being arrested for auto theft is one thing. Adding an interstate drug charge to it and my wife and I could spend our retirement years in Florida. In prison.

While the Sheriffs talked among themselves, I thought back to the day when a couple of neighborhood friends and I made a really bad decision. On a stupid dare we hot-wired a car. Drove it with no registration. No license. And clearly no sense. We were 16. A few blocks later the car stalled. We jumped out and ran like hell.

The Sheriff finally returned to our car and informed us that it was our license plate that was stolen and switched, most probably to cover up some other crime. They removed our plate and had us return the car to the nearest Avis/Budget location....a twenty-minute ride. Annoying but certainly manageable.

And then I had a chilling thought. What if we were people of color instead of retired white folks from Connecticut. In this part of Florida our little inconvenience might have resulted in the dire consequences we read about everyday.

To paraphrase the old Avis advertising slogan ---We all need to Try Harder.

33

DELICIOUS

T hen there was the time that my dad dated his aunt. I should explain.

When my mother passed away my dad was greeted with a long line of casseroles. Brandished by widows of all shapes and sizes.

My dad was a great catch. He had his own teeth. Most of his hair, less a small hole in the back of his haircut. And, drumroll please....he could still drive at night.

But my dad had no more interest in the women that came to the door or in the casseroles and sad stories they brought with them.

This was a guy who didn't have a lot of friends. No social network. No hobbies. He hadn't had a date since World War II. My mother oversaw their social life. Now that she was gone, he was clueless. And a lot lost.

Anyone who knows anything about people of an advanced age would not be betting on too many future candles on his birthday cake. My siblings and I grew increasingly concerned.

And then the phone rang.

My Great Aunt Sylvia called to check in on him.

Let me describe Sylvia. She was a spitfire of a woman barely 5 feet tall. Her husband, my Uncle Nat, passed away a year or so earlier. What time she had on her hands was in a word...filled. She was a woman in constant motion. Continuously on the phone with family and friends. She was in everyone's business. She edited the community newspaper. And was always available to volunteer for a good cause.

Everyone loved Sylvia.

To be clear. Sylvia was my mother's aunt. She became my father's aunt BY MARRIAGE. I didn't want to make it sound like we were from somewhere in the back woods where cousins marry each other and play banjoes on their front porch.

Sylvia and my dad spoke several times a day. And their relationship grew.

To Sylvia anything that was wonderful was called DELICIOUS. It was her favorite word. Because almost everything in her life felt so wonderful to her. She was incredibly positive.

Her many friends were delicious. Books she enjoyed were delicious. Music she listened to was delicious. In fact, until I received a wedding invitation I thought her granddaughter, Daniella, was named Delicious. Because that was the only name by which I knew her.

My dad who was in his late 80s would drive from Long Island to her home in New Jersey. He would hop on the Long Island Expressway and head up through the Bronx over the George Washington Bridge and then onto the New Jersey Turnpike for a while.

If you haven't already shivered with fright, reread the last sentence. That is the scariest drive imaginable -- at any age. We all became increasingly concerned because my dad was a rather laissez-faire driver. No real accidents to speak of but his 10-year-old Buick - a classic grandpa car - had more dings and dents than a golf ball.

It took a few more years for us to wrestle his driver's license away. Once we found someone who could drive him to Sylvia's, we all breathed a sigh of relief.

When my wife Norma and I were married at a resort in Cancun, Sylvia and my dad attended. They had separate -- but adjoining -- rooms. How 1940s of them.

Sylvia went to the market in Cancun. It's a bit of a tourist trap. But you can get great deals on jewelry, trinkets, and souvenirs if you are willing to negotiate with the merchants. That is all part of the fun.

Sylvia picked out a small piece of jewelry to bring home. When the merchant gave her the price, she said that couldn't be the right price. So, he lowered it as one might do when negotiating.

Sylvia, ever true to her far left political leanings, then explained that this was much too low a price to pay and that she didn't want to take advantage of him. She offered to pay him 50% more of what he originally asked. The deal was quickly completed, and the word spread.

For the rest of her time in the marketplace she was treated like a visiting dignitary or a rock star. Everywhere she went she was greeted by throngs of eager merchants.

That was Sylvia.

A few years later age caught up to them both. But the last of their long lives were extended with hearts that were full right up to the end.

I learned two things from their relationship.

First, you are never too old to fall in love.

And, second, if you see the world as full of wonderful things that are delicious, your life will be that much sweeter.

My dad with Sylvia proving that you are never too old to fall in love.

34

FRIENDS SINCE EISENHOWER

I cannot remember much of my life before my friends George and Stuart came into it. We were 6 and in the first grade at PS 176 in Queens.

Everything in our world back then was big and moved fast. We were the little guys. Our older siblings were well established in elementary school. They were the big kids. They had friends and book bags and knew their way around. They also wanted nothing to do with us.

We were awkward, goofy looking and clumsy. To them we were an embarrassment. Not cool to be around. So, they kept their distance as we began our school days trying to find our place in the new and confusing world called the first grade.

What we found was each other. Three clueless guys on a mission to survive and grow up.

Over the decades we've been there for each other's first fights and first kisses. Through the wilds of puberty and the crazy times in junior and senior high school. We even found ourselves together in a high school fraternity that brought a new dimension to our friendship.

As the years passed there were graduations and weddings. The births of children. The loss of parents. And a hundred other bumps, bruises and celebrations along the way.

A long way. Thirteen Presidents long. Friends for over 65 years.

Though we now live in other areas of the country we are still in each other's lives. On the occasions when we are physically together, we act like the 17-year-old idiots we once were.

The challenges of aging are put on hold for a time, to allow for childlike laughter and joy. And to remind us that life, though sometimes messy, is also wonderfully sweet. A little like eating chocolate cake with your hands.

They get a little extra kick out of reading my stories. For the most part, my stories are their stories too. They participated in many of the antics of my youth. And these experiences created a bond among us.

I am so very lucky to have them in my life.

I'm not one to offer advice. Getting through my own life is enough of a challenge. We all have a friend or relative we haven't spoken with in a while. Don't wait. Pick up the phone and reach out. It might just enrich both of your lives.

*Recent photo of George, Stuart and me. In the inset photo I'm
seated on the left. George is standing behind me. And Stuart
is standing on the right.*

ACKNOWLEDGMENTS

I would like to thank my beautiful wife Norma who reminded me of stories I had long since forgotten. She took the first stab at editing as this book began to take shape. And she did her best to correct my bad habit of using prepositions to end my sentences with.

My brother Andy, my best friend since diapers – though we tried to kill each other more than a few times - helped me remember the small details of our lives together. This book would not have been possible without his edits, guidance, encouragement, and good memory.

My dear friend of forty years, Geno Paesano, reminded me to write in my own voice. *"You ain't Hemingway! Cut it out and get back to your voice,"* still echoes in my head.

Lastly, I'd like to thank Colleen Brunetti of Bannon River Books, LLC who coached me through the often confusing, self-publishing process. Her guidance and support were invaluable to me.

ABOUT THE AUTHOR

Eric Litsky was born in the Bronx and raised in Queens in the middle of the post-war, baby boom years. After his tumultuous college years at the University of Hartford in CT he had a 10-year career in advertising/public relations followed by three decades as a commercial real estate broker.

Between his careers and raising a family, Litsky has been an amateur singer/songwriter, tango dancer, stage actor, musician (tuba player) and now an author.

He resides with his wife Norma in Northern CT.

Litsky Muses On Writing

I suppose if I had a "do over" (a mulligan if you are a golfer), I would have flossed more often and spent much more time with my grandparents listening to their stories......about their times, about their lives. But like all youngsters, I was too busy being a kid.

Rarely does a young person have the patience or the curiosity to hear stories from older person's life. Having four grandchildren was all the encouragement I needed to write.

As I wrote I found I had more to talk about. And that my stories would entertain and be relevant to those of all ages and all walks of life. The details in the oral history of one's family fade over time. If nothing else, I hope that your reading of my stories not only entertain but encourage you to take your own pen to paper. And share the moments that shaped your life with the people you care about.

I believe that the greatest gift we have is not our collection of tchotchkes or other property. It is our stories. For who we are is the compilation of the stories of our lives. Although each story in this book is true and exactly as I was able to recall, I did take the liberty of changing some names. If you do recognize yourself in any of these stories, it is probably you. In which case I'm sorry. Or you're welcome.

Also by Eric Litsky

Harry Would be So Proud: A pocketful of funny and heart-warming stories

Available on Amazon in hard cover, soft cover and Kindle.

"Litsky's book is highly readable and often delightful, with plenty of general reminiscences of everyday life undergirded by the sense of optimism that many people had in the immediate post-World War II decades." - Kirkus Review

Written in the same rollicking and reflective tones as *Frying Pork Chops Naked*, Litsky's debut book brings you thirty-three funny and heartwarming stories. A few snippets to whet the appetite...

Home Cooking: *"There was the time my grandmother nearly killed my entire family. She took a half-cooked brisket to Brooklyn for my cousin Matthew's bris. It was an hour ride from the Bronx on an un-air-conditioned subway. Her plan was to finish cooking the brisket when she got there. Science had other ideas. It nearly wiped out three generations of our family in a single July afternoon..."*

My Bar Mitzvah: *"Today I am a man," I said in a vocal range that ran from high alto to low baritone. All within the same sentence. I had a little peach fuzz on my upper lip. And my puberty hormones left me with a perpetual boner..."*

Keep in Touch

www.EricLitsky.com

www.ingramcontent.com/pod-product-compliance
Lightning Source LLC
Chambersburg PA
CBHW060540130626
46553CB00002B/836